Guide to

Mount Kenya
and
Kilimanjaro

Part One
General

Published by
Mountain Club Of Kenya
P. O. Box 45741, Nairobi, Kenya.
1998

Designed and Produced by Alpha Graphics Ltd
P. O. Box 47694 Nairobi, Kenya.

Printed by Préci-ex Ltd - Mauritius

First Published (Editor Ian C. Reid), 3 impressions
October 1959

Second Edition (Editor Ian C. Reid), completely revised
October 1963

Third Edition (Editor John Mitchell), completely revised
October 1971

Fourth Edition (Editor Iain Allan) completely revised
December 1981

Reprinted with revisions and corrections October 1990
Reprinted with revisions and corrections October 1998

ISBN 9966-986-0-3
Library of Congress Catalog Card No. 90-980316

Cover Photograph:
Mount Kenya from Teleki Valley
Photo by Ulf Carlsson

Distributors:

The Mountain Club of Kenya
P.O. Box 45741, Nairobi, Kenya

Designed and produced by *Alpha Graphics Ltd*
Tel: 531578   .   P O Box 47694

CONTENTS

Topographical Diagrams of Selected Routes on:

PART THREE: KILIMANJARO

Climbing on Mount Kilimanjaro

LIST OF PLATES

MAPS and DIAGRAMS

FOREWORD

It is seven years since the Mountain Club of Kenya updated its
authoritative guide to Mount Kenya and Mount Kilimanjaro.
While most of the information remains relevant, some signifi-
cant changes have occurred. These new changes have now
been added in their respective chapters.

This revision is the collective effort of a number of Mountain
Club of Kenya members. Some of the sections have been
updated to take acount of the changes that have taken place
since 1990.

The Mountain Club of Kenya
October 1998

Halford Mackinder.   A painting by Fredrick Beaumont.   1941

Part One
General

MOUNTAIN MEDICINE FOR
MOUNT KENYA AND KILIMANJARO

Brent A Blue, MD
and
Alastair R L Stevenson, BDS

Introduction

Climbing Mount Kenya and Kilimanjaro has unique medical implications. Mount Kenya, known for its steep faces and rapidly rising altitude, has claimed as much as 50% of all the high altitude pulmonary oedema cases in the world each year. Kilimanjaro, because of its easily accessible tourist route, exposes large numbers of non-technical, less prepared climbers to high altitude. Both mountains can be safe, but preparation must be made to ensure safety. Epics are easier to prevent than extricate oneself from: a strong prevention pro-gramme has significantly reduced mountain sickness cases in Kenya. A little planning could save yourself and others being involved in an unnecessarily dangerous situation. Persons attempting to climb Mount Kenya and Kilimanjaro should be in excellent physical condition with a reasonable goal being the ability to run five miles in forty-five minutes. There are no absolute medical contra-indications to climbing to altitude except for certain cardiac and pulmonary diseases for which effected persons should consult their physician. Good condi-tioning will allow the climber to enjoy his work at altitude, with-out being totally fatigued.

Additional preparations also include enough food, water and protection from the element, these should be well thought out. Climbers should consume three to four litres of fluids and eat approximately four thousand calories of food a day. Most estimates by exercise physiologists rate consump-tion of calories at five thousand per day for most climbers, but weight loss will be inevitable as it is almost impossible to force this many calories down. Appetite tends to fall away and the planned menu must be especially appetising to entice one even to cook it. With the potential luxury of being able to hire porter, a menu with fresh meat, vegetables and fruit should be considered. A diet high in carbohydrates seems to help reduce symptoms of acute mountain sickness and increase the blood oxygen levels as well as being high in calories. It is best to consume carbohydrates for breakfast and lunch, proteins at night. A craving for acidic fruit, due to an initial blood alkalosis form Co^2 lost in hyperventilation, makes tinned fruit and fruit drinks invaluable. A large variety of fruit flavourings is also conducive to increasing fluid intake and preventing dehydration.

This guide, coupled with up-to-date local knowledge, will enable fairly accurate planning of an itinerary, hut, routes, number of days, etc., to be left with the park authorities (it is a requirement that this itinerary is entered in the entrance gate log). This can be of particular importance off the tourist route on Kilimanjaro. Mental attitude prior to commencing a climb is most important. Failure is usually more frequent than success on most hard technical climbs and "success at any cost" can kill without reason. A proper frame of mind and mental attitude on the mountain are critical.

Any climbing, except for solo ascents, requires team thinking. Establish good communication between team member and set known goals. Every team individual will have personal desires and these should be honestly expressed and "aired" prior to ascent. Much tension and hostility can thus be avoided.

The Elements

Cold can cause problems ranging from minor discomfort to deadly hypothermia. Preparation is the best solution. A person should always dress in layers so that proper ventilation can be achieved. It is easy to become over-heated while climbing, which produces large amounts of respiration, causing dehydration and a wet body and clothes. Stopping physical activity in such a condition can be a "chilling" experience; also the temperature change between sunlight and shade, day and night, is large and acute, so have extra warm clothes available.

When climbing, if large amount of sweat or heat build-up occur, a layer of clothes should be shed immediately. Some climbers will find that they climb in shorts and T-shirt, but have to rest wearing a heavy parka or wool sweater. It is worth noting that wool will keep you warm when wet, as will artificial fibre pile and fleece materials.

Three major routes of heat Loss occur:

1) by evaporation, which is mainly lost by wind blowing across the body, so use a wind-breaker.

2) by conduction, where heat is lost by sleeping directly on the ground, to prevent this loss use an insulation pad like closed-cell foam or an air mattress.

3) by radiation, which is best controlled with reflective materials, hats should be worn. The old adage is "cold feet, put on your hat". A person can lose 40% of his or her body heat via the head because the vessels of the scalp cannot constrict in response to cold, thus losing valuable warmth.

There are two serious forms of cold pathology - frost-bite and hypothermia.

Frostbite

Frostbite is the destruction of soft tissue, usually in the fingers and toes, secondary to the freezing of fluid into crystals in and around the cells of the tissues. Its initial presentation is whitening of the skin. It then turns red and feels hard. Frostbite is usually accompanied by numbness and a tingling sensation. Blisters and darkening of the skin are later signs. Prevention is the key. Good wool mittens (warmer than gloves because of physical limitations of the insulation properties of an individually wrapped finger), with overmitts are important. Wool socks and good mountaineering boots (not hiking boot), with water repellent applied to the boots are also critical. Some may consider double boots for serious ice routes.

Frostbite treatment has been recently reappraised.

In general, rapid rewarming in hot water (38°C - 43°C), is suggested; however this should only be done when the effected part can be kept warm. Recent evidence has shown that much frostbite damage occurred because of freezing. Doctors now suggest that frost-bitten feet, for instance, be kept stay cool preventing the cycle if rescue cannot be made. In addition, tissue damage is increased if affected areas are used after warming. Frost-bitten parts should not be used if possible.

Once rewarming occurs, the injured parts should be gently cleaned with antiseptic soap as for burn therapy. Sterility is emphasised blisters should not be opened and absolutely no cutting of dead tissue should be done. It may take six months to a year to determine if a finger or toe is viable. All persons with frostbite should be seen by a qualified doctor as soon as possible.

Hypothermia

Hypothermia can be much more insidious and deadly. Hypothermia is the lowering of the body's core temperature (temperature of the major internal organ). Hypothermia is considered mild to 35°C, moderate to 32°C, and severe at less than 32°C. A person can go from normal to severe hypothermia very quickly, particularly if immersion in cold water occurs. Although they can be tremendously uncomfortable, cold feet and toes do not indicate hypothermia, as they do not accurately reflect core temperature. Unfortunately regular fever thermometers do not work well in these temperature ranges.

Predisposing factors include improper ventilation and layering of clothes, allowing oneself to become wet from rain or perspiration, inadequate clothing, exhaustion and starvation. The first signs of hypothermia are shaking chills and mental, emotional and intellectual dulling. A person with these symptoms should be kept active and warmed with additional clothing, and near a fire or other heating source. Hot liquid, although psychologically good, have no real temperature changing effect. Alcohol may be a morale booster, but any

more than one or two ounces is contra-indicated, as it can complicate the hypothermia. Placing the person in dry clothes and a warm sleeping bag in a protected area (e.g. tent, bivouac sack, or cave) is very effective. If hypothermia proceeds shaking chills usually cease. This is a clue to increasing severity of hypothermia, and the patient will not recover without external warming.

If a person has moderate hypothermia, he should be immobilised and immediately warmed (there can be rapid progress to severe hypothermia and unconsciousness). Placing the person into a sleeping bag with one or two others can be effective. Clothing should be removed from everyone in the sleeping bag to allow direct skin-to-skin contact (no time for modesty). A heating source, if available, would be most important.

People who are found in moderate to severe hypothermia should be immobilised because the effect of blood from the extremities returning to the core can cause cardiac arythmias (irregular heart beats). Severe hypothermia is usually caused by cold water immersion, burial in an avalanche, or severe long-term exposure to the elements. It is usually heralded by disorientation, confusion and lethargy.   The patient may be comatose and mimic death as his temperature falls below 27°C. A person is not dead until he is "warm and dead". The general consensus now is not to begin cardiac pulmonary resuscitation or warming until the patient is in a controlled environment such as a hospital. Rapid rewarming and administration of drug without proper control of the patient can be deadly, mostly due to cardiac arythmias.

Obviously if facilities are more than six hours away a decision must be made. The patient, when this cold, is in a sort of a suspended animation, and "rocking the boat" could be worse than doing nothing.

To prevent such emergencies, the technique of controlled bivouacking is important to learn. If bivouac is a possibility, a bivi bag, preferably Goretex and a good quality sleeping bag are essential when embarking on any of the technical route. Knowing when and where to stop and how to use available materials and features to gain protection form wind and rain, minimises the discomfort, maximises the rest, and prevents hypothermia.

Hypoxia; Fluid Balance and Acclimatisation

Hypoxia is low oxygen in the air, which occurs with increasing altitude. This is reflected in the body by low oxygen in the blood called hypoxemia. This is usually noticeable above 3,500 metres and is marked above 5,000 metres. It is herald by shortness of breath even with mild exertion. The body responds to hypoxemia by acclimatisation. There are three physiological effects of acclimatisation. The most immediate change is due to a chemical being released to help the blood free more oxygen for the tissues. Secondary but slower effect is an increase in the blood count which allows the blood to carry more oxygen. (This increase takes up to six weeks to reach maximum, but it also increase the problems of clotting disorders like thrombophlebitis). Finally the climber will increase ventilation and cardial response to low blood oxygen.

To aid acclimatisation and prevent any of the specific high altitude diseases, the most important factor is rate of ascent. Paced steps are important and rest when exertional shortness of breath occurs. Be ruled by your breathing at altitude rather than your leg muscles, as at low altitudes. With hypoxemia, thinking may be slowed and some coordination lost, which is fortunately reversible with descent! Try to walk from below 3,000 metres; do not necessarily take transport as high as possible. Above 3,500 metre try to average 500 metres altitude gain per day. Take an extra acclimatisation night every third day or 1,000 metres gain (as from the Meteorological Clearing to Teleki Valley and on the Naro Moru Route)

It is the altitude at which one sleeps that is critical, so plan the day backward form the height at which you need to sleep, and try to ascend above the height during the day. With increasing altitude and decreasing temperature, humidity falls to a low level. This results in insensible fluid loss from the respiratory passages. One to two litres can be lost each day even at moderate altitude. The resulting symptoms such as dry mouth and nose, sore throat and tender sinuses, are best treated by forced intake of fluids, together with cough or throat lozenges and inhalation of steam. Dry air can also predispose to viral infections and cold symptoms. As part of the acclimatisation process, mucus secretions are increased to combat this drying. Panting should be avoided, and sweating controlled by adjusting clothing layers. With the decreased availability of water at high altitude, dehydration is a real threat.

Urine output is a good gauge of dehydration. Small amounts of dark yellow urine indicate dehydration. The lighter and the larger the volume, the better the hydration. "Clear and copious", should be the watch-words, (at least 1 1/2 litres of urine output per day). An added advantage of correct fluid intake is that it also seems to aid acclimatisation, and is important, if the acute mountain sickness symptom of deceased urine output develops, to rule out the possibility that it is due solely to dehydration.

Dehydration usually occurs concurrently with acute mountain sickness and oedema of the lungs and brain.

Specific High Altitude Diseases - AMS, HAPE, HACE
Specific high altitude diseases are divided into three categories:
1. Acute mountain sickness (AMS);
2. High altitude pulmonary oedema (HAPE);
3. High altitude cerebral oedema (HACE).

Current medical thought is that high altitude disease is related to decreased breathing while sleeping at altitude. Thus, the adage, "climb high, sleep low". It is known that at high altitude many climbers hear their tent mates breathing periodically, with long pauses between breaths ('Cheyne-Strokes breathing"). This is considered normal, within limits, but thought to be related to mountain diseases.

Acute mountain sickness is the most frequent high altitude disease, and is a failure to acclimatise. Symptoms include headache (common), nausea, vomiting, anorexia, fatigue, insomnia, swelling of hands, feet or face (peripheral oedema), and decreased urine output. Nearly all climbers will have some of these symptoms. Persons with severe symptoms should stop ascending and consider descent for a few days. Examples of severe symptoms would be a headache unresponsive to aspirin and a night's sleep, decreased urine output, and persistent nausea and vomiting. They can be reduced or prevented by slow ascent and acclimatisation. Diamox (acetazolamide), mild diuretic, has a side effect of preventing decreased rate of breathing during sleep and can be helpful in preventing acute mountain sickness. It is not a substitute for slow ascent or acclimatisation.

Why a small percentage of climbers get the potentially deadly high altitude pulmonary oedema or high altitude cerebral oedema is unknown. The most common single denominator is rapid ascent without acclimatisation. HAPE and HACE have not been shown to be associated with sex, race, physical conditioning, or previous symptom-free high altitude work.

Pulmonary oedema is heralded by increased shortness of breath even at rest, gurgling breath sounds (rales), which can be heard with an ear directly placed on the chest (they sound like hair being rubbed together next to the ear), and sometimes the production of frothy white sputum. The patient usually has cough and may produce this sputum, blood-tinged. Always assume with these symptoms high altitude pulmonary oedema until proven otherwise and do not make the mistake of treating just for pneumonia.

High altitude cerebral oedema is heralded by severe headache and uncoordination. Hallucinations frequently occur, but are usually denied. There are several medical diagnostic signs but only a couple which do not require equipment for testing:
1) A headache unresponsive to aspirin or acetaminophen with codeine.

2) Ataxia (uncoordination).
The test for the latter is heel-to-toe walking in a straight line. All persons will have some problems with this at high altitude due to cold and clumsy boots, so have a second person walk the line for comparison with the possible HACE patient. If a person cannot walk a competent heel-to-toe straight line, he is considered to have HACE until proven otherwise.

In researcher Peter Hackett's words there are three treatments for HAPE and HACE..."descent, descent, descent". Sometimes as little as 500 metres can make a tremendous difference. Treatment must be immediate. It is all-right to allow the patient to walk if he can, but if he cannot, he must be carried down. Severe cases (all cases of HACE) should be carried to medical help.

All other treatments are only holding measures. Oxygen can be used if available but is no substitute for descent. A rate of about two litres a minute is necessary over an extended periods (12-24 hours), to be of any value. A "blast" for five or ten minutes is useless.

Many drugs, heart stimulants, diurectics, steroids, analgesics, have been used but none has consistently shown any obvious benefit. Concentrate on descent and evacuation.

After a couple of days of acclimatisation at low altitudes, a slow re-ascent may be tried.

Other Mountain Related Condition

Exhaustion: Obviously, both mental and physical exhaustion are part of mountain climbing. Physical exhaustion can be minimised by forcing eating; neither of which are pleasant at high altitudes. Adding curry or cayenne pepper to food can usually encourage intake of fluid in most climbers. Mental exhaustion is tougher to prevent and treat. It is important to be in good psychological shape, but setbacks and fatigue can frustrate a person into depression. Forcing oneself to carry out a regular routine of duties at all altitudes seem to add some sense of stability, which can help.

Mount Kenya. Halford Mackinder at the Summit 13th September 1899

Feet: Probably the most common and painful mal-adies in the mountains are sore feet and blisters Prevention here is also the best approach. Boots should be well broken in and two or three pairs of socks should be worn. Some prefer wearing tennis or running shoes up to the actual base of a technical climb, or until cold conditions are reached.

Blisters occur from rubbing between skin and the surrounding materials. Socks reflect the motion of the boot. The climber should attend to painful areas at the very first sign, even if it is five minutes out of camp. The best therapy at the first sign of blister is to cover the area completely with one single layer of plain adhesive tape (zinc oxide porous type is the best), and it should be left there until the end of the trip. Adhesive foam can be used, but the climber must know the proper technique or the foam can create additional problems. Adhesive foam should be used with the principle of spreading the pressure over a large surface area. It is usually best to prepare the skin for tape or adhesive foam with benzoin solu-tion which makes the skin tacky.

Descending the mountain usually creates problems for the toes. Jammed toenails and blisters on top of the toes are very common. Toenails should be kept as short as possi-ble. When going down, the top of the boot should be laced as tight as possible to prevent the jarring of the foot into the end of the boot, It is not unusual to have numbness in the toes due to them being jarred in the boots and the effects of cold. Sensation normally returns after a few weeks.

Lacerations and Abrasions

When a laceration (cut), or abrasion (scrape), occurs on the mountain, there are two main treatments:
1) Pressure on all bleeding sites; this will stop bleeding if held long enough.
2) Scrubbing the area well with plain soap and water; antibac-terial soap is best, but any soap will do.

Preferably do not place creams or ointments of any kind on cuts or abrasions. They make the wound moist and slow healing. Besides, they do virtually nothing to kill bacteria. It is generally agreed that no suturing on the mountain is necessary, and in fact may be a source of infection by closing in dirt and bacteria. Wounds heal better clean and dry no matter how big. Plastic surgeons can always revise a scar but septicemia (blood poisoning), from a sewn-over cut can be deadly.

Sunburn

The strength of the tropical sun is easily underestimated. Its destructive U.V. rays penetrate cloud and are more powerful with increased altitude; snow is also a very effective reflector (70% to 90%). This reflected light is the most damaging as it often strikes normally unexposed skin, such as the nose and chin. The lips, neck, and the backs of the knees are also very vulnerable sites.

All protection is in the form of barriers: silk scarf for lower face and neck, hat, beard, long-sleeved shirt, long socks, etc. Of the commercial sunscreens, the ones containing para-amino benzoic acid (PABA) or PABA esters (such as Pabanol, Pre Sun), are the most successful. Choose one with a high sun protection factor (5% or No. 6 at least), and apply before exposure to sunlight and at intervals depending on the degree of sweating.

Snow Blindness

This is a U.V. burn to the eye surface, the cornea. It produces blistering of the cornea, swelling of the conjunctiva (inner eyelid), intense pain and temporary loss of sight. In an emergency, anaesthetic drops relieve the pain and so restore sight, but the eye becomes extremely vulnerable to foreign bodies. The eye should be padded and bandaged for up to 48 hours as soon as possible. Cold tea make soothing eye drop. Prevention is achieved by wearing goggles or dark glasses with side-shields. In an emergency cardboard with tiny slits tied round the head will suffice.

Trauma (Violent Injury)

Some simple rules:

1) Check breathing, pulse and then reassure the patient.

2) Prevent further injury.

3) Keep warm and dry (feed and hydrate).

4) Splint for fractures, both for comfort and to control internal breathing (it may hurt severely to straighten a fractured leg, but it may save a litre or two of blood loss internally; many lives were saved during World War II by the simple use of the newly invented Thomas Splint which kept broken femurs straight).

5) Climber rarely need or request pain medication. Once given, it decreases the injured climber's ability to cooperate or make decisions.

6) Send for help if someone is available and give complete information on the situation.

7) Make realistic decisions about what to do. In a party of two, an injured climber may have to be left alone in order to get help He may be dead by the time help returns, but had the partner not left for help, there may have been two bodies, instead of one.

8) Traumatic injuries which cause cessation of breathing or heartbeat are almost always fatal regardless of the location, and a real assessment of recovery should be made before endangering the lives of other members of the party.

9) Recovery of bodies is the last priority when compared to the survival of the rest of the party.

Splints can be made form ice axes, backpack frames, and host of other materials Most stabilisation procedures require thought and a little creativity.

Personal First Aid Kit

The contents of your personal first aid kit are only of use if you know what each item is used for, and how and when to use it effectively. It is pointless to carry syringes and ampoules up the mountain, if you are not prepared to administer them to yourself or others. Knowing how a medication effects the user is most important.

Plan the kit so that:

1) Everything has as specific purpose, or two (e.g. Codeine - pain and diarrhoea).

2) Everything is well labelled (someone else may need to use your kit on yourself).

3) Everything is insufficient quantities to be useful (remember to replenish used items).

You can purchase ready made kits and tailor them to your needs, but it is often better to prepare your own, and a comprehensive list of contents is included here. Obviously individuals and small parties will not wish to carry the whole range of items listed and should select those to take according to their particular circumstances.

Make sure that it is all packed in a uncrushable, waterproof container and try to include some notes or signs, symptoms and treatment of the more common mountain ailment and trauma injuries. Sod's Law says that this guide will not be accessible when needed!

Suggested first Aid Kit overleaf.

Suggested Reading
(1) *Medical care for Mountain Climbers*: Peter Steele; Heinemann.
(2) *Medicine for Mountaineering*: James A Wilkerson, MD; The Mountaineers.
(3) *Mountain Sickness*: Peter H. Hackett, MD; American Alpine Club.

DRUG	EFFECT	MAJOR SIDE EFFECT
(1) Antihistamine Benadryl (diphenhydramine) 25 mg. Dose: 1-2 every 4-6 hours. OR Piriton (Chlorpheniramine) 4 mg. Dose: 1 every 6-8 hours.	1. Dry up nose. 2. Anti-allergic symptoms. 3. Allergic reaction to plants and strings. 4. Sedations (no hangover). 5. Anti-nausea/vomiting.	1. Sedation, mild. 2. Dry mouth and nose.
(2) Decongestant: Sudafed (pseudephedrine) 30-60 mg every 4 hours.	1. Dry up nose and sinuses.	1. Make slightly hyper.
(3) Anti-diarrhoea: Imodium (loperamie) 2 mg 2 tablets immediately for loose stool; 1 after each loose bowel movement. No more than 8 per day. OR Lomotil (2nd choice) 2.5 mg. 4 tablets immediately. Then 2 tablets every 6 hours.	1. Stops diarrhoea.	1. None. 1. Blurred vision, fatigue.
(4) Aspirin and Paracetamol as required	1. Headache 2. Fever 3. Minor aches	1. Minor stomach upset
(5) Aspirin and Paracetamol with Codeine 30 - 60 mg every 3-4 hours.	1. Moderate pain 2. Sedation 3. Anti-diarrhoeal	1. Can cause headache with large amounts of usage 2. Some cold intolerance 3. Mild sedations 4. Altitude may increase effect
6) Cough and Throat Lozenges	1. Dry sore throat.	1. None

DRUG	EFFECT	MAJOR SIDE EFFECTS
7) Broad Spectrum Antibiotic: Keflex (cephalexin) 500 mg. Dose: 1 three times a day. OR Erythromycin 500 mg. Dose: 1 four times a day.	1. Bacterial infection: Systemic or local with spread	1. Some diarrohea 2. Some nausea. 3. Vaginitis. 4. Possible allergy.
8) Canesten Cream (clotrimazole).	1. Athletes Foot 2. Jock Rot 3. Manilial (fungal vaginitis).	1. Possible local allergic reaction.
9) Valium (diazepam) 10 mg. OR Dalmane\(flu-razepam) 30 mg	1. Heavy sedation.	1. Hangover. 2. Sedation 3. Decreases breathing rate
10) Sun Block: 5 % Paba based skin preparation and lip preparations.	1.Prevents sunburn at altitude. (should be put on 30 minutes prior to exposure)	1. None. Sometimes local irritation
11) Strapping and bandages. 2" Adhesive tape. Gauze Rolls and pads	1. Can be used for anything from blisters to sprained ankles, to fixing a pack frame, to making splints.	1. Sometimes people allergic to this material
12) Dental: Eugenal	Place on cotton and (oil of clove) hold on sore tooth. Numbs.	1. Taste
13). Opthalmic: Neo-Cortef (hydrocortisone and neomycin) 2-3 drops 3 times a day	1. Conjunctivitis. 2. Snow blindness (the only true cure for snow blindness is patching the eyelids closed for 24 or more hours). 3. May also be used for outer ear infections.	1.Do not use if possible, viral infection of eye.

DRUG	EFFECT	MAJOR SIDE EFFECTS
14). Water Sterilising tablets: Sterotabs, 1-2 tabs/litre or as otherwise instructed	1. Water purifying (wait 30 minutes)	1. Taste
15. Tincture Iodine.	1. Washing wounds. 2. Sterilises skin.	1. Stains
16. Dulcolax (bisacodyl) 2-3 tablets a day.	1. Strong laxative. 2. Stool softener	1. Strong stomach cramps.
17. Tropical: Fluorinated Steroid cream. Rub small amount in well 3 to 4 times a day.	1. Good for skin rashes 2. Haemorrhoids. 3. Mosquito bites. 4. Eczematous-type rashes	1. Not for use on wounds 2. Excessive use (over 2 weeks) on face as mucus membranes can cause skin atrophy
18. Rectal: Anusol Suppositories/cream. (1 per rectum as necessary).	1. Will help shrink haemorrhoids.	1. None
19) Astringent Pads, eg. Tucks or Wash n' Dri.	1. Peri-rectal hygiene	1. None.
20). Insect repellent	1. Prophylactic against insect bites	1. None
21) Anti-malarial: Chloroquine 250 mg. 2 tablets once a week on the same day each week	1. Malaria prevention	1. Some nausea. 2. Itching
22) Mountain sickness: Diamox (acetazolamide) 250 mg. 1 twice a day	1. Thought to be helpful for prevention of HACE and HAPE 2. Prevention and treatment of symptoms of AMS 3. Peripheral Oedema (swelling).	1. Causes mild increase in urination 2. Intermittent tingling sensation in fingers and toes.

THE GLACIERS OF MOUNT KENYA AND KILIMANJARO

Stefan Hastenrath

Department of Meteorology, University of Wisconsin

During the Pleistocene, glaciation on Mount Kenya
and Kilimanjaro may have reached down as far as about 3,000
metres. Ice sheets thus covered much of the Mount Kenya
massif as well as the Saddle and Shira Plateaus of Kilimanjaro.
Geomorphic evidence on the glacial history of the two mountains according to Baker (1967), and Downie and Wilkinson
(1972), is summarised in Table 1. The highest moraines of
either mountain are still completely bare, devoid soil formation,
and colonisation of boulders by lichens has hardly had time to
take place. Late Pleistocene glaciers began to retreat around
15,000 years ago at about 3,000 m in the Aberdares, and
around 11,000 years ago at about 4,200 m on Mount Elgon
(Hastenrath, 1984). Absolute dating of Late Pleistocene to
early Holocene glacial events on Mount Kenya and Kilimanjaro
is still lacking.

Examples of the various moraine stages given in the
table for Mount Kenya are found near the Naro Moru track:
stages I and II in the ascent before reaching the height overlooking the Teleki Valley.
Stages III in the area where the footpath descends into the valley.
Stage IV to VI upward of Mackinder's Camp.
On Kilimanjaro the sequence of corollary moraine complexes
can be observed on the southern flank, near the Umbwe route
and Mweka route.

A more detailed chronology of glacier behaviour has
been compiled for the time interval since the end of the 19th
century (Hastenrath, 1975, 1984). For Mount Kenya, (Fig. 1
and table 2), reports and photographs from the early expeditions (Gregory, 1984; Mackinder, 1900), reveal that glaciers
reached close to the innermost large moraines at the end of the

19th century. A pronounced recession of all glaciers - the Barlow Glacier on the Northwest face of Point Pigott, the Kolbe Glacier Northeast of Point Lenana, the Melhuish Glacier to the Southwest of Point Melhuish, and four other glaciers have disappeared altogether. A remnant of the former Melhuish Glacier still existed in 1978. Several mountain lakes, such as Harris, Lewis, and Tyndall Tams, have been vacated by ice in recent decades, and new moraines have since been formed, e.g. below Tyndall Glacier.

The Lewis Glacier, the largest ice body on Mount Kenya is the object of a multi-annual field study currently underway, and aimed at a quantitative understanding of long-term glacier variations in terms of the climatic forcing. Lewis Glacier is unique in all the tropical belt in that a continuous historical documentation of its long-term behaviour is provided by mappings in 1985, 1982, 1978 and 1974 (Caukwell and Hastenrath, 1982; Hastenrath, 1984); in 1963 (Forschungsunternehmen Nepal-Himalaya, 1967); in 1958 (Charnley, 1959); and in 1934 (Troll and Wein, 1949); and the photographs of the Mackinder expedition in 1899. A network of stakes laid out on the glacier serve to monitor the spatial pattern of net balance and the surficial ice movement (Hastenrath, 1983, 1984). The continuity of this network is being maintained under great difficulties, and the cooperation of considerate visitors in protecting this monitoring programme will be much appreciated.

The Lewis Glacier shrank steadily from 0.60 square km in the 1890's to 0.26 square km in the 1982. The elevation of the terminus rose from 4,465 m to about 4,600 m in the same period. The total volume loss seems to have been most drastic in the early part of the century. The total ice volume is estimate at more 35 million cubic metres in 1982. Maximum ice flow velocity at the turn of the century was, from numerical modelling, estimated to about 15 metres per year, while in 1982 the observe velocity was only about 3 metres per year.

In the Kilimanjaro massif, only Kibo is presently glaciated, (Fig. 3 and table 3). A rapid ice recession is under

Mount Kenya. Point Lenana and the Lewis Glacier

Ian Howell

Jaeger, 1908; Hastenrath, 1984). On the eastern rim of Kibo, a way, as in other high mountains of East Africa (Meyer, 1900; continuous ice wall existed at the end of the 19th century, but much of this area is now ice-free. The early explorers christened a series of glaciers on the southern flanks of Kibo by German names. Separate ice tongues that existed at the beginning of the century have lost definition. Only the tongue of the Heim Glacier at the western end of the "Southern Ice Field" still appears distinctly. The remnants of the Ratzel Glacier at the eastern rim of Kibo are separated from this ice field and they are disintegrating rapidly into separate entities. The same applies to several bodies of ice in Kibo crater. to the west and north of the "Southern Ice Field", in the area of the Great Breach, there are some smaller glaciers in a state of gradual decay. A large and continuous body of ice, the "Northern Ice Field" extends along the northern crater rim, with distinct glaciers, descending far down the western lopes of Kibo. Unlike Mount Kenya, the ice fields of Kibo often display an ablation form of irregular towers and pinnacles, known under the name "nieve de los penitentes" Low atmospheric humidity and the distance away from the equator area factors in the origin of the phenomenon.

Marked asymmetry is apparent in the ice distribution. On Mount Kenya, the largest glaciers extended to the southwest of the mountain. On the Kibo cone of Kilimanjaro the formally low-reaching glaciers on the southern flanks as opposed to the north side can be understood from differential insulation resulting from the location of the mountain in the southern hemisphere. However, the contrast between the eastern crater rim, ice-free up to 5,800 metres, and the western slopes of Kibo, where the glaciers descend to around 4,800 metres, is even more pronounced. The east-west asymmetry on Mount Kenya and Kilimanjaro is related to the strong diurnal circulations.

The multi-annual field programme on Lewis Glacier combined with computer simulations (Hastenrath, 1984; Kruss,

1983) has led to a quantitative reconstruction of the climatic causes of glacier recession in East Africa. A decrease in annual precipitation of the order of 150 mm and associated cloudiness and albedo variations during the last quarter of the 19th century, followed by a secular air temperature rise of a few degrees centigrade during the first half of the 20th century, are identified as the major climatic forcing of the observed glacier response. Some of the important climatic forcing are too small to be measured by conventional meteorological sensing techniques. Therefore, glacier observations are essential in monitoring long-term climatic change in the tropics.

TABLE 1. Glaciation phases and moraine stages at Mount Kenya and Kilimanjaro (according to Baker, 1967; and Downie and Wilkinson, 1972). Numbers indicate typical lower limits of moraines.

MOUNT KENYA	KILIMANJARO
Retreat to present position Little Ice Age (2 stages), VI, A, B, 4,600 m. Deglaciation. Retreat, 4 stages recognised, II - V, 4,000 - 4,300 m.	Retreat to present position Recent Glaciation (2 Stages) 5,200 - 4,600 m. Possible deglaciation. Little Glaciation, "Upper" and "lower" 4 stages, 4000 m
	Interglacial?
Younger Maxima, 4 stages 1 A -D, 3,400 m.	Fourth (main) Glaciation, 2 stages, 3,400 m.
	Interglacial
Older Glaciation	Third glaciation; first and Second Glaciations

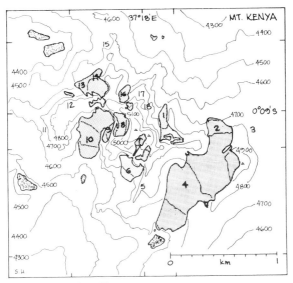

Fig 1 Glaciers of Mt. Kenya

Table 2. Nomenclature of glaciers on Mount Kenya.
Numbers refer to the map.

1. Krapf
2. Gregory
3. Kolbe
    (disappeared after
    1926)
4. Lewis
5. Melhuish
    (disappeared after
    January 1978)
6. Darwin
7. Diamond
8. Forel

9. Heim
10. Tyndall
    (disappeared)
11. Barlow
12. NW Pigott
13. Cesar
14. Joseph
15. Peter (disappeared after 1926)
16. Northey
17. Arthur (disappeared)
18. Mackinder (disappeared)

27

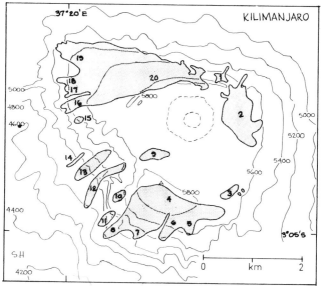

Fig 2. Glaciers of Mt. Kilimanjaro

Table 3. Nomenclature of ice entities on Kibo. Numbers refer to the map.

Asterisks denote new, and brackets alternative names.

1	Eastern Ice Fields *	12	Great Barranco
2	-		(Big Breach)
3	Ratzel Glacier	13	Little Barranco
4	Southern Ice Field		(LittleBreach)
5	Rebmann Glacier	14	Arrow
6	Decken	15	Uhlig
7	Kersten	16	Little Penck
8	Heim	17	Great
9	Furtwangler (Western Crater)	18	Drygalski
10	Diamond	19	Credner
11	Balletto	20	Northern Ice Field

References:

Baker B. H. 1967: *Geology of the Mount Kenya area*. Geological Survey of Kenya, Report 79, Nairobi, 78 pp.

Caukwell, RA. Hastenrath, S. 1977: *A new map of Lewis Glacier, Mount Kenya*. Erdkunde, 31, 85-87.

Charnley, F., 1959: *Some observations on the glaciers of Mount Kenya*. J. Glaciol, 483-492.

Forschungsunternehem Nepal-Himalaya, 1967: Mount Kenya 1:5,000. Kartographische Ansalt Ferytag-Berndt und Artaria, Wein.

Gregory, JW., 1984: *Glacial geology of Mount Kenya*. Quarterly. Journal Geol. Soc., 50,515-530.

Hastenrath, S., 1975: *Glacier recession in East Africa*. p. 135-142 in WMO-IAMAP Symposium on long term climatic variations. August 1975, Norwich, England, WHO No. 421, Geneva.

Hastenrath, S.,1977: *Fluctuations of Mount Kenya glacier*. p. 14, 80, 105, 119, INIUGG-ICSI-UNESCO, Permanent Service on the Fluctuations of Glaciers 1970-75 vol. 3 UNESCO, Paris, 269 pp.

Hastenrath, S., 1983: *Net balance, surface lowering, and ice flow pattern in the interior of Lewis Glacier, Mount Kenya,* J Glaciol., 29,392-402.

Hastenrath, S.,1984: *The glaciers of equatorial East Africa*. Reidel, Dordrecht, Boston Lancaster, 353 pp.

Jaeger, F., 1909: *Forschungen in den Hochregionen des Kilimandscharo*. Mitteilungen aus den Deutschen Schutzgebieten, 22,113-146,161-197

Kruss, P., 1983: *Climatic change in East Africa*: a numerical simulation from the 100 years of terminus record at Lewis Glacier, Mount Kenya. Zeibschrift fur Gletscherkunde und Glazialogeologie, 19, 43-60.

Mackinder, H., 1900: *A journey to the sumit of Mount Kenya, British East Africa. Geog.* Journal, 15, 453-487.

Meyer, H., 1900: *Der Kilimandscharo*. Dietrich Reimer, Berlin, 436 pp.

Troll, C., Wein, K., 1949: *Der Lewisgletscher am Mount Kenya*. Geografiska Annaler, 31, 257-274.

THE CLIMATE OF MOUNT KENYA
AND KILIMANJARO

Stefan Hastenrath

Department of Meteorology, University of Wisconsin

The large-scale circulation over East Africa is characterised by a double passage of the Equatorial Trough, with a
north-easterly monsoon flow prevailing over the Indian Ocean
during the northern hemispheric winter, and a south easterly
flow at the height of the northern Summer. The resulting rainfall regimes in eastern Africa are manifold. In Central Kenya
there are two main rainy seasons, the so-called "long rains"
from mid-March to June, and the 'short rain" form October to
late December. However, weather disturbances and precipitation can occur at any time of the year. The most likely periods
of fair weather on Mount Kenya are:
1) mid-January to late February, and less so
2) late August and September.
In north-eastern Tanzania, the main rainy season lasts from
March to May; only a weak secondary maximum indicated in
December.

The mean annual elevation of the $0^{\circ}C$ minimum,
mean and maximum temperature in the free atmosphere over
East Africa is around 3,500 m, 4,750 m, and 6,000 m respectively. The annual temperature range is about $2^{\circ}C$, with the
lowest values in March-April and highest in July-August. As
common in low latitudes, the diurnal temperature range is
large, amounting to about $20^{\circ}C$ in January-February, and about
$12^{\circ}C$ in July-August.

On Mount Kenya, the wettest sector is on the outcast
slopes of the massif, with up to 2,500 mm per year, whereas
the driest part, the "treeless gap" to the north may receive less
than 1,000 mm per year. An altitudinal belt of maximum rainfall
lies around 2,700 - 3,100 m with amount decreasing towards
the peak area. A stratiform cloud deck tends to hover between

2,800- 3,800 m. Above about 4,500 m most of the annual precipitation falls in solid form. During the rainy seasons, the peak area is often covered in snow, with depth on the glaciers of one metre and more, and crevasses in the glacier are not visible. As a result of insolation conditions, the southern slopes of the mountain become snow-free during the December-March "dry" season, whereas in July-October the north face becomes bare.

On Kilimanjaro the largest rainfall amounts are received on the southern slopes of the massif, facing the southerly monsoon. The altitudinal belt of maximum precipitation may lie below 2,000 m with annual totals of more than 2,000 mm. Precipitation decreases drastically towards higher elevations, with values dropping to less than 250 mm per year on the desertic Saddle Plateau. A stratiform cloud deck is frequently found with an upper limit around 3,000 - 3,500 m; the peak areas above the altitudinal belt may be in bright sunshine. In contrast to Mount Kenya, water supply in the higher parts of the massif may be a difficult proposition during the dry season; even the chances of finding snow patches below the level of the glaciers may be poor.

As is common in the higher mountains of the Tropics, diurnal circulations are vigorously developed, with wind blowing down the mountain from evening throughout the night into the middle of the morning, and a reversal to upslope flow from then into the afternoon. Very strong winds are quite regularly encountered in the peak area in the early morning, speeds gradually decreasing after sunrise. The meso-scale circulation mechanism dominates atmospheric events on the mountain, liability for cloudiness, mist and rainfall being greatest between about 11 am and 5 pm. As a consequence, westward facing slopes tend to receive less insolation than those of easterly aspect. In the peak regions, clearing often sets in rather abruptly about one to two hours before sunset. Awareness of the strong diurnal control of weather phenomena is found helpful in the planning of mountaineering ventures.

Reference:

L H Brown, J Cocheme, 1973: *A study of the agroclimatology of the highlands of Eastern Africa.*

W.H.O. Technical Note No. 125, W.H.O. N0. 339, *Geneva*, 197 pp.

East Africa Meteorological Department, 1970: *Temperature data for stations in East Africa, parts I-III, Nairobi.*

Kilimanjaro. Giant Groundsel.   *David Keith Jones*

THE ECOLOGY, FLORA AND FAUNA OF MOUNT KENYA AND KILIMANJARO

Truman Young
Department of Biology, University of Miami

The geological anomaly of glaciers on the equator is paralleled by the biological paradox of the term 'tropical alpine'. The unique climatic stresses of equatorial high elevation have produced a unique flora and fauna, which have attracted the attention of biologists from all over the world.

With increasing elevation, temperature steadily decreases, at a rate of about 5 degrees centigrade per thousand vertical metres. Cold air can hold less moisture than warm air, so as air cools it tends to lose its moisture as rain. The wet weather in East Africa tends to come from the east and south-east, producing the following pattern of rainfall on high mountains. Warm moist air from the east encounters the mountains and begins to rise over them. This air cools and rain falls. This is why the eastern and south-eastern slopes of Mount Kenya and Kilimanjaro are the wettest slopes. By the time the air reaches elevations above 4000 m, most of the moisture has been extracted, and these highest areas are characteristically very dry.

These changes in temperature and rainfall are reflected in changes in the flora and fauna as none ascends the mountains. The lowland habitats surrounding East Africa's mountains are hot and dry. Most are grasslands and thorn scrub and used mainly as rangelands. On the gentle lower slopes of he mountains, a cool moist climate combines with rich volcanic soils to provide excellent agricultural land.

As recently as 100-400 years ago (depending on the site), this land was covered by diverse indigenous forests, which lived hunter-gatherers, such as the Dorobo and the now-extinct Gumba. The relatively recent arrival of local agriculturist resulted in the conversion of the forest to farms that play a major role in feeding the people of East Africa. This agricultural expansion was eventually limited by increasingly steep slopes at higher elevations, and by the creation of Forest Reserves. Both colonial and modern independent governments recognised the value of these forests as watersheds and as sources of forest products. The lower limit of indigenous forest on Mount Kenya and Kilimanjaro now mainly stands at 2,000 - 2,500 metres.

East Africa's mountains have been visited by outsiders for less than one hundred years, and only sporadically. Therefore, many plants do not have common English names, unless they have close relatives in Europe. Most of the forest trees have local (Kikuyu, Meru, Chagga, Dorobo) names, but in the little-visited areas above the treeline, often the only plant names are scientific.

The Montane Forest Zone

The montane forests of Mount Kenya and Kilimanjaro vary considerably, with wetter forests on the southeastern slopes and drier forests on the northern slopes. In fact, the northern slopes of Mount Kenya are so dry around Timau that the forest there is broken up into isolated patches, producing a gap in the belt of forest that has allowed migration of grassland animals between the lowland and alpine zones. However, Kilimanjaro is generally the drier mountain.

The dominant tree on the northern slopes of both mountains is the pencil ceda (Juniperus procera), a shaggy-barked tree with scale-like leaves. It attains tremendous girth and heights of over 30 m. Along the Sirimon track on Mount Kenya, these giant cedars and other trees are scattered in a very open grassy forest that allows much greater visibility than other forest areas.

Perhaps the most characteristic tree of East African montane forest is podo (Podocarpus milanjianus). Like cedar, podo is a heavily-exploited softwood timber tree, and a relative of pines. It produces robust narrow leaves that litter the forest

35

floor, where you can also find the fruits of podo. These are small hard green berries, often with a flesh red aril. The latter is edible and tasty, and the fruit is dispersed by monkeys, turacos, and hornbills.

There are many other species of forest trees, of which the most common include African olive (Olea africana), Schefflera and Nuxia congesta. Olive can be recognised by its deeply pitted trunk. It is most common at lower elevations and in drier forest. Schefflera trees start as epiphytes and eventually kill their host trees, as strangler figs do. The resulting tree is often misshapen. It has palmately compound leaves just as in the house plant of the same name. Schefflera is found in many forests, but is particularly common along the upper Machame track on Kilimanjaro. Nuxia is a tall tree with a dark trunk. The Mandara track on Kilimanjaro has some massive tree, although this species is found in all mountain forests.

Because walking off the track into the forest is dangerous and often prohibited, mountain visitor see mostly trackside plant and animals. The common shrubs include elderberry (Sambucus africanus), Vernonia, and raspberry (Rubus).

Elderberry has big compound leave, masses of small white flowers, and dark edible fruits. Vernonia has small blue flowers and seeds with white fluff. Raspberry is unmistakable with it sharp prickles, rose-like flower, and orange to red raspberries. Watch also for begonias especially on Kilimanjaro. They may be vine or free-standing shrubs or small trees, and have showy white two-lipped flowers.

There are many colourful herb along the forest tracks. The flowers that look like clover are just that (Trifolium). The small blue pea flower with trifoliate leaves is Parochetus communis. The big yellow flowers flat on the ground are sunflecks (Guizotia reptans). There are many species of Impatiens flowers, looking vaguely orchid-like. Most are pink, but species occur that are white with purple specks, one that is bright red. the orange-red species common on Kilimanjaro (Impatiens kilimanjaro) is found nowhere else. The tall mint with balls of orange flowers is one of the lions paw mints (Leonotis spp). The tall blue mints are Plectranthus spp. Beware of stinging nettles (Urtica massaica), whose leaves look just like the blue mint', but are infinitely more painful.

The birds of the forest are shy, but worth seeing. Hartlaub's turaco is most obvious when it show its flash of brilliant red in the wings as it flies from tree to tree. The big silvery-cheeked hornbills and red-fronted parrots occur at fruiting tree. The scaly francolin is not uncommon along the tracks. Other birds include olive thrush, mountain buzzard, black-capped waxbill, malachite sunbird, tacazze sunbird, cinnamon-breasted bee-eater, black rough-wing swallow, white-headed wood hoopoe, fiscal shrike, Ruppell's robin chat, and the dueting hunter's citicola. On Kilimanjaro watch for the broad-ringed white-eye. Mount Kenya's Met Station is visited by two rare birds - the green ibis (flying over at dusk and dawn) and the Abyssinian ground thrush.

Forest mammals are rarely seen. More visible species include black-and-white colobus monkeys, Syke's monkeys, bushbuck, buffalo (but not on most Kilimanjaro tracks), and at lower elevations, baboons and waterbuck. The rooting holes along Kilimanjaro tracks are made by bush pigs. Watch for signs of elephants on Mount Kenya - droppings and tusk marks in the road cuts. Rarely seen also are black-fronted duikers, leopards, sunis, giant forest hogs, genets and hyenas. the curious wail of the tree hyrax is characteristic of nights spent in the forest. The dirt mounds on the mountains are the result of excavations by mole rats. Zebra can be seen in the open Sirimon forest.

The Bamboo Zone

On Mount Kenya, but not on drier Kilimanjaro, a band of bamboo is a conspicuous component of wetter forest. These stands are natural, and not the result of disturbance, as is usually the case elsewhere in the worlds. Bamboo forms dense stands that appear impenetrable from the roadside, but are very open underneath. The numerous game trails there should explain the necessity of taking a ranger if you wish to explore the forest on foot. Bamboo stands usually have few species because they effectively suppress other plant. Individual stands of bamboo grow and spread for many years, then flower synchronously and die back to begin the cycle again. The bamboo belt occurs at intermediate elevations, with podo forest above and below.

The Timberline Forest

Near the upper limit of true forest, smaller tree pre-dominate. These are sometimes scattered amongst glades to give the appearance of parkland. The two characteristic trees here are African rosewood (Hagenia abyssinica) and giant St John's wort (Hypericum). The rosewood has big compound leaves and pendulous clusters of small flowers. Its trunk is often misshapen and festooned with mosses and hanging goat's beard (Usnea).

The Hypericum has small leaves and large yellow flowers. Wildflower abound. Red-hot poker (Kniphofia thom-soni) occurs here alongside true violets (Viola spp). The giant forest lobelia (Lobelia bambuseti) has multiple stems up to 3 metres tall, each with a terminal rosette of leaves. Some of these will be bearing tall cylindrical inflorescences. Pink Impatiens are common here.

High Altitude Heathland and Chaparral

Timberline occurs at 3,000-3,500 metres, being lower at drier sites. Above this more or less distinct timberline, the habitat is characterised by shrubs with small leaves. In moister sites, these are mostly heathers (Erica and Phillipia), some of which grow to over 10 metres and form dense stands that are virtual forest in themselves. Drier sites are characterised by shrubbier plants that are often aromatic. These include African sage (Artemisia afra), pea-flowered Adenocarpus mannii, sug-arbush (Protea kilimanjaro) with its thick leaves and white head-like flowers, straw-flowered shrub everlasting (Helichrysum chionoides), and the slender green Euryops brownei, with bright yellow flowers. Fires are not uncommon here, especially in the drier sites, which can be appropriately called tropical alpine chaparral. The herb layer includes gentians (Swertia spp), sedges (Carex spp), and several alpine species common higher up.

The animals that occur here are a mixture of forest and alpine species, with two conspicuous exceptions form lowland savannah bush. Alpine chaparral is home to herds of eland and occasional lions. Eland tracks and droppings, and occasionally elands themselves, can be seen above timberline at Sirimon on Mount Kenya, and on both the saddle and the Shira Plateau on Kilimanjaro. The rhino that once lived here are now all gone.

The Afro-alpine Zone

With increasing elevation the high altitude heath and chaparral gradually give way to true afro-alpine vegetation. The chaparral, which occurs in drier areas, tends to be more extensive than the heath, but both disappear by about 3,800 metres.

Tropical alpine areas experience a unique climate. The thin dry air at high elevations result in a striking pattern of daily temperature fluctuation. Because this air provides little barrier to incoming sunlight during the day or to outgoing heat at night, plants and animals experience dramatic warming in the morning and freezing temperatures after sunset. Olav Hedberg described this pattern as "summer every day and winter every night." This pattern is even more striking in the tropics than in the temperate zone, because in temperate alpine areas the nights are relatively short during the growing season (the summer), and the sun is less vertical. Alpine existence may well be more rigorous on the equator than in Europe or North America.

One consequence of this daily temperature fluctuation is a process called solifluction. Nightly freezing produces needle ice in the soil that pushes up the surface dirt. The morning sun thaws the needle ice, allowing the soil to fall back down. This daily churning of the soil uproots young seedlings, leaving the ground bare in 'solifluction deserts'.

One strategy to deal with this ever-churning soil is to abandon rooted life and float atop the tumult. Several lichens do this, a well as the remarkable moss balls, which roll with every day's upheaval. Moss balls are one example of the special plant growth forms that are found in tropical alpine habitats

The most spectacular of these are the giant rosette plants, characterised by dense leaf rosettes resembling cabbages or artichokes. Unrelated giant rosettes occur in tropical alpine areas around the world, and are excellent examples of convergent evolution. In East Africa there are three kinds: Carduus, Senecio and Lobelia. The giant thistle (Carduus keniensis) is found only on Mount Kenya and the Aberdares.

Giant groundsels (Senecio) are found only on East African mountains. Their rosette leaves are always large and up to 10 cm wide. Some species have stems. On Mount Kenya there are two tree groundsel. The most common is Senecio keniodendron, which grows as tall as 6 metres. This species has green-backed leaves that are retained after they die and form a dense insulating layer around the stem. It is most common at higher elevations (above 4,000 metres) on dry slopes. The other tree groundsel on Mount Kenya is S. battiscombei. It's pale-backed leaves are only rarely retained around the stem, giving this species a narrow stemmed appearance. It is less common (not found in the Teleki Valley) and occurs at lower elevations in moister sites. These two tree groundsels are represented on Kilimanjaro by close relatives: Senecio jonstonii and S. kilimanjari respectively.

The cabbage groundsel (Senecio brassica) produces patches of white-backed rosettes close to the ground. It occurs in wetter sites on both mountains. In addition to the giant groundsels, there are numerous herbaceous species of Senecio.

Mount Kenya. Cheque left on the Summit of Nelion by Eric Shipton and Wyn Harris recording the first three Ascents.

All have small bright yellow flowers and are very similar to the groundsels of the northern hemisphere. Mount Kenya is home to three alpine giant lobelia rosettes can be distinguished by their narrow lance-like leaves, and the bitter milky latex that flows from wounded parts. In all giant lobelias each rosette grows for many decades, then produce one large inflorescence and dies.

In Lobelia telekii (the 'ostrich plume lobelia'), which produces a feathery flower stalk up to 3 metres high, the entire plant has only one rosette, and so an individual plant flowers only once at the end of a long vegetative life. This species occurs on Mount Kenya (but not Kilimanjaro) in dry sites.

The other giant Lobelias have many rosettes, and so live on to flower more than once. Lobelia aberdarcia is found only near the tree limit above Timau on Mount Kenya. Lobelia deckenii is found on both mountains, and is the only alpine giant Lobelia on Kilimanjaro. Its geometrically elegant flower stalks are often shredded by the feet of birds that visit the pretty hidden flowers. Its leaf rosettes contain water that freeze into small crescent every night, hence the nickname gin-and-tonic Lobelia. This water is not just collected rain, but is actually produced by the plant itself. Because the water never freezes solid, the submerged leaf bud is protected form freezing. Lobelia deckenii differs from mountain to mountain, and the Mount Kenya form is also known as L. keniensis.

Another special plant growth form is the giant grass tussock. There are several species of afro-alpine tussock grasses and sedges, two of which are dominant. In wetter sites Festuca pilgeri forms extensive dense waist-high grassland that is almost impenetrable. In drier sites, and especially on Kilimanjaro, Pentaschistis minor dominates. It is a much less robust grass, and characteristically forms rings.

The small green shrubs with toothed leaves are Alchemilla. There are many pretty afro-alpine wildflowers. There are several species of everlastings (Helichrysum spp), which can be recognised by their dry, white to pink flowers.

They are most common in drier site. Afro-alpine buttercups (Ranunculus orephytus) can be recognised by their shiny yellow flowers with five petal. This is a flat rosette plant of wetter sites. Another is the sunburst (Haplocarpha rupellii), with its showy multi-petalled yellow flowers. The bright red African gladiola (Gladiolus thomsoni) occurs at lower elevations. There are over 100 species of alpine wildflower on Mount Kenya and Kilimanjaro, and you will see some in flower, whenever you visit.

The alpine animals of Mount Kenya and Kilimanjaro are many and varied. Luckily, it is too high for bees, wasps, fleas, and mosquitoes, but there are many interesting insects, especially butterflies in the dry season. Aside from a few timberline frog, it is too cold for amphibians. Similarly, there are few reptiles, but you may see the Afro-alpine lizard sunning itself in grass tussocks, and above Timau there is a chance to see the small rare Hinde's viper. Introduced trout of several kinds now thrive in Mount Kenya's streams and tarns.

Birds are common. Jackson's francolin and African snipe occur in the lower alpine, as does the dueting warbler, hunter's cisticola. Tacazze sunbirds and scarlet-tufted malachite sunbirds visit flowering lobelias. Streaky seedeaters and mountain chats are frequent camp visitors on both mountains, and on Kilimanjaro white-napped ravens are. Alpine swifts are commonly seen overhead, and pied wagtails work the waterways. Birds of prey include Augur Buzzards (some of which are black), Verreaus's eagles (which specialise in catching hyrax), Mackinder's eagle owls, and the rare lammergeyer. Slender-billed chestnut-winged starlings regularly come up form the forest to visit Mount Kenya's alpine Lobelias, and in years of mass flowering will nest high on the mountain. Black ducks live on several of Mount Kenya's tarns. The alpine areas of both mountains are also frequented by local, regional, and European migrants.

There are several kinds of rodents, but most are not seen by the visitor. However, vole-like groove-tooth rats are like to be seen scurrying along their well worn paths during the day. They appear to be the staple of both leopards and birds of prey. They are particularly common in the Teleki Valley on Mount Kenya. At the trash pits at Horombo Hut on Kilimanjaro, they can be seen alongside striped grass mice. The night time chattering nuisance in some of the hut is the African dormouse, easily recognised by its furry tail.

Of particular interest is the Mount Kenya rock hyrax. Hyrax are a taxonomic anomaly distantly related to elephants. Alpine rock hyrax occur only on Mount Kenya. Unlike their relatives the tree hyrax, rock hyrax live in colonies in rocky areas. They are particularly common in the moraines near Mackinder's Camp. They have a rich vocabulary and a mischievous nature. Do not feed them or leave food where they can find it, because they inflict nasty bites and are enterprising thieves. Feel free to watch them from a distance, for they are fascinating.

Grimm's duiker is a small buck resident above treeline. Wandering eland may be seen throughout dry areas, and regular alpine visitors include Zebra, Buffalo, Elephant, and Hyena. All but the Zebra have been seen above 4,500 metres. Anomalous fatal visits to the high alpine have been recorded for bongo, Syke's monkey and black-and-white colobus.

Leopards are the only large carnivores common in the high alpine zone. Their droppings and tracks are more often seen than they are. However, they do travel before sunset and sometimes prowl around huts and campsites, so you may be lucky enough to see or hear one. They are not dangerous if left alone. Some of the alpine leopards are black. The frozen leopard on top of Kilimanjaro is interesting, but not unexpected.

Leopards regularly traverse high passes in their wanderings. Leopards, lions and spotted hyena have all been seen near the summit of Point Lenana on Mount Kenya, and an entire pack of wild dogs on the crater rim of Kilimanjaro. Man is not the only mountain climber.

Mount Kenya. Rock Hyrax.   *Joe Cheffings*

References:

Coe, M J 1967 *Ecology of the alpine zone of Mount Kenya* Junk
Publishers, The Hague.

Hedberg, O 1964. *Features of afro-alpine plant ecology..* Acta
Phytogeographica Suecica 49: 1-144.

Smith, A P and T P Young. 1987. *Tropical alpine plant ecology.* Annual
Review of Ecology and Systematics 18: 137 - 158.

Young, T P and M M peacock. 1985. *Vegetative key to the alpine
vascular plants of Mount Kenya*
J E Afr. Nat. Hist. Soc. 187: 1-9

CLIMBING STANDARDS

There is plenty of excellent walking and scrambling on both Mount Kenya an Kilimanjaro. But, even the simple routes (e.g. Point Lenana or the normal route to Gillman's Point), must be treated with care. It cannot be stated too strongly that bad weather or bad judgement can turn a friendly mountain into an exceedingly dangerous one in a few minutes.

Climbs on rock and ice should only be attempted by those experienced in the use of a rope, ice-axe etc.; and in each party attempting the climbing routes at least the leader should have considerable mountaineering experience under all conditions.

A numerical system of grading is used on the mountains of East Africa. This operates form grade I to VI, with an additional grade of VII to indicate the very technical rock routes which have been climbed recently on Mount Kenya. This grading system works to its best advantage where rock routes are concerned, and these climbs are graded after the hardest pitch on each route. Ice routes, however, need an explanation.

Many ice route, particularly on Mount Kenya, follow steep couloir which are frequently exposed to rock and ice falls. So these route have been given gradings of VI to show to climbers the overall seriousness of the climb - not the technical difficulty. For example the technical difficulty of the Diamond Couloir does not exceed Scottish IV, yet it is graded VI. This is because it is a natural funnel for any debris avalanching off the upper section of the Diamond Glacier. There is therefore, no way the Diamond Couloir could be graded IV.

The suffixes "sup" and "inf" have been used to indicate climbs high or low in their grade. A few aid routes have been climbed, and these are graded A1, A2, A3, or A4.

It should be noted that these grades are given for routes when they are in top condition. They will undoubtedly be higher for climbs attempted out of season, or in abnormal

Mount Kenya. View from Teleki Valley as photographed by Mackinder's expedition 1899.

conditions. Ice conditions are likely to vary considerably.

Times needed for climbs naturally vary according to conditions, the ability of the party, etc.; but those given are the approximate average needed for the ascent only by a two-man rope, from the foot of the climb to the summit. It is recommended that parties should bear in mind that all routes on Batian and Nelion should be regarded as two-day climbs; and some Kilimanjaro route on the south-west side of Kibo can be multi-day climbs.

When considering times and lengths of climbs and probably making estimates from alpine experience, two additional factors should be borne in mind: the altitude - Austrian Hut is almost the height of the summit of the highest peak in Europe - and the short equatorial hours of daylight, averaging 12 hours of daylight throughout the year.

In keeping with good practice, a proper climbing helmet is recommended for climbs on rock and ice. Stonefall does occur, although the rock is generally sound.

In the description of routes, directions are given facing the climb, unless otherwise stated.

The gradings correspond approximately to French, English and American grades as follows:

East Africa	French	English	American
I	F	Easy or Moderate	5.1-5.2
II	P.D	Mod. or Difficult	5.3
III	A.D	Diff. or Very Diff.	5.3-5.4
IV	D	V. Diff. or Mild Diff	5.5
V	T.D	Severe or Very Severe	5.6-5.7
VI	E.D	V.S. or Hard V.S.	5.8
VII	E.D+	Extreme	5.9-5.11

Part Two

Mount Kenya

THE GEOLOGY OF MOUNT KENYA

Nayan Bhatt
University of Nairobi

Introduction

Beginning in early Tertiary times (about thirty to forty million years ago), parts of Eastern Africa began to experience strong upheavals of the earth, caused by deep-rooted geological processes. These processes seem to be similar to those which created the Red Sea and the Gulf of Aden by the drifting away of the Arabian Peninsula from Africa. These upheavals spread progressively southward through Ethiopia, Kenya and beyond to Lake Malawi.

The main manifestations of these deep-rooted processes are the arching up of the ancient foundation rocks, extensive flooding by lavas through fissure, volcanic eruptions, and splitting of the earth's crust. At least three circles of the above series of events can be recognised as having occurred within the last twenty-five to thirty million years. These geological events led to the formation of dome-shaped high volcanic plateau in Central Ethiopia, Central Kenya and Western Uganda, all three cut along their crust by the Great African Rift Valleys. At Afar in Ethiopia, the northern end of the main Rift Valley forms a triple junction with the Red Sea and the Gulf of Aden, suggesting a link with the formation of Oceans and Continental drift.

Thus the rise of high mountains in Eastern Africa is the consequence of volcanicity and Rift Valley formation. Many volcanic cones and craters, mostly dormant but in few cases active and various stages of preservation, can be seen on the rift floors; examples of these are Longonot, Susua, Menengai in Kenya, and the active Lengai in Tanzania. The Aberdares and the Mau ranges are fissure volcanoes of the rift shoulders. The highest summit are formed by volcanoes which are situated one hundred to one hundred and fifty kilometres east and west of the main rift, i.e., Mount Kenya, Kilimanjaro, Mount Elgon and Mount Meru. The Ruwenzoris and the Usambaras are ancient non-volcanic rock massifs up thrusted along the rift faults

MOUNT KENYA

The commanding topographic feature in the Kenya highlands east of the Rift Valley is Mount Kenya; a large central type volcano whose summit stands at 5,199 metres above sea level. It was built up by intermittent volcanic eruptions, mainly in the period 3.1 to 2.6 million years ago. Flank eruptions of lavas, related to the Nyambene volcanic hills to the north east of Mount Kenya, continued to within the last 40,000 years.

The base of the volcano is a little over one hundred kilometres in diameter and rests on an ancient and irregular erosion surface that occur about 1,500 metres above sea level. Originally the summit of Mount Kenya must have reached well over 6,500 meters. The maximum total thickness of volcanics exceeded 5000 meters, thus producing a volume in excess of 3,700 km^3. Since then about 35% of this volume has been removed, mainly by glacial erosion on the upper part of the mountain. Of the remainder of this succession only six hundred metres is exposed in the alpine zone. The rest, amounting to some three thousand metres of succession, remains hidden from observation.

Mount Kenya displayed a cyclic pattern of volcanic behaviour with periods of violent activity alternating with longer periods of quiescence. It is likely that each cycle of eruption commenced with the explosive shattering of the main crater region, followed by eruption of fluid lava, thus forming a sequence of fragmental material and lava sheets. The ensuing period of calm must have been of sufficient duration for weathering and the river systems to become established.

Occasionally the magma at depth, unable to rise through the main vent due to its being effectively plugged, found its way t the surface via parasitic cones and craters.

Except for cones and craters formed during the waning life of the volcano, most of the earlier vent structures are buried below the lava sheets from the main vent.

The fragmental rocks formed by the explosive shattering of the crater region at the commencement of each cycle were blown high and wide. The larger fragments settled near the vent area while the finer fraction dispersed widely. Thus, these rocks, which are called agglomerates, are thicker and coarser near the vent, and thin progressively at greater distances away. On the other hand, the fluid flows of lavas, whose course were dictated by existing depressions and valleys, are thinnest and glassy, due to rapid chilling, on the steeper slopes near the vent. They then thicken progressively outward and away form the vent on the gentler slopes, where they are better crystallised.

PHYSIOGRAPHY

When viewed form a distance, the two physiographic zones of Mount Kenya are quite apparent: the lower forest covered or cultivated slopes; and the abruptly commencing open moorlands, which pass upward to alpine terrain; the transition between the two takes place at an altitude of roughly 3,300 metres.

1. The Lower Slopes: The gradient of the lower slopes is almost parallel with the dip of the underlying lavas. A system of radial streams has incised these slopes down to a depth of two hundred metres, leaving broad, smooth ridges. However, towards the moorlands, the drainage changes to a denser sub-parallel stream pattern due to higher rainfall, and the ridges are narrow and steep.

The region of lower slopes between the Nithi and Sirimon rivers is distinctly different with the ground gently undulating and with fewer streams. It is covered by porous volcanic ashes and agglomerates, and is characterised by numbers of volcanic necks, cones and explosion craters. The notable examples are: Ithanguni, reaching over 4,000 metres, with its crater occupied by Lake Alice; two circular stock-like bodies forming smooth elevated platforms known as Giant's Billiard Table and Rutundu; and numerous recent basaltic cones and craters.

2. The upper slopes: The moorlands have relatively gentler slopes but they steepen considerably in the alpine zone, starting at about 4,300 metres. Extensive glaciers once reached down to the moorlands, and their remnants have now retreated to the central peaks. Such typical features of glacial erosion as U-shaped valleys, various kinds of moraines and ice-smoothed surfaces are seen in the moorlands.

The alpine zone is characterised by the diminishing ice-sheets, ice-worn cliffs, screes formed by frost-shattered rocks, and almost a total absence of vegetation. This alpine zone commences at the cirques formed the heads of U-shaped valleys, and encompasses the precipitous central group of peaks. Outer peaks like Tereri, Sendeyo, and Point Lenana, occur at the intersections of ridges bounding three or more cirques. these ridges, which are generally serrated, also carry high pinnacles like The Tooth, Thomson's Flake and Point Thomson. The inner group of peaks including Batian, Nelion and Point Pigott, are formed from the massive, highly resistant plutonic rock which forms the plug of the main vent.

Many beautiful tarns occupy the depressions formed by glacial excavations, and dammed by moraines and craters.

ROCK TYPES

Rocks are composed of minerals which form by the following processes: from magma; subsequent alteration by heat and pressure in the earth's interior; chemical breakdown by weathering. Most rock-forming minerals are complex compounds of silica and metals. The lighter metals, like sodium, potassium and aluminium, give colourless or light-coloured minerals, while heavier metals like magnesium, iron and titanium give dark-coloured minerals. In addition, rapidly formed minerals are generally microscopic or small in size, while slowly crystallised minerals are large. The manner in which a rock is formed determines its group, i.e. igneous rocks from molten magma; metamorphic rocks form alteration by heat and pressure; and sedimentary rocks by cementation of the residual mineral deposits formed after weathering of existing rocks.

Igneous rocks formed from molten magma erupting on the surface are called lavas. These are frequently glassy due to rapid chilling but subsequently may alter to reveal microscopic crystals, i.e. become devitrified. However, many lava flows contain varying amounts of large crystals especially of light-coloured varieties, and the resulting texture is known a porphyritic, with each individual crystal called a phenocryst.

Molten magma which crystallised slowly below the surface, insulated form sudden heat losses, as in dykes or volcanic necks, shows a texture of large interfering crystals known as plutonic.

The important light-coloured or colourless minerals in igneous rocks are quartz (silica), feldspars (sodium, aluminium, potassium compounds of silica), and feldspathoids (like nepheline, which are chemically similar to feldspars but poorer in silica). Zeolites are alteration products of the silica-deficient nepheline group of minerals, which are typically found filling bubble cavities or vesicles of lavas.

The important dark-coloured minerals ranging form black to brown in colour, are olivine, proxenes and amphiboles.

The igneous rocks are broadly divisible into three groups based on silica content. The acidic or rhyolite-granite group have abundant quartz (free silica), and are generally lighter in colour. The intermediate or trachyte-syenite group have traces of free silica and are moderately dark. And finally, the basic or basalt-gabbro group are dominated by dark minerals with subordinate feldspars so that the rocks are almost black. The presence of feldspathoids suggest even greater deficiency of silica.

Phonolites, kenytes and nepheline syenites are chemically related intermediate rocks, which contain sodium-rich lighter-coloured minerals, including the characteristically waxy nepheline. The differing textures of these three rocks are due solely to their differing rates of cooling and crystallisation.

Trachytes are lighter than phonolites and belong to the more normal intermediate group of rocks. Feldspar in these rocks dominate over the dark minerals.

All of the above rocks are subjected to atmospheric and mechanical weathering when exposed at the surface, and these produce subtle hues, distinctive patchy colouration, characteristic mineral alteration products, and fracture joints geometrically related to the structure and form of the rock body.

The magmas tapped by the majority of volcanoes in Kenya and its borderland with neighbouring countries, are classified as alkaline, and give rise to a series of rock types whose minerals are rich in sodium and poor in silica. These magmas originate in the earth's interior, below the continental crust at depths of fifty to sixty kilometres, and rise through deep fractures in contrast to oceanic magmas which have much shallower sources. Thus the minerals of alkaline rocks, and their chemistry, are quite distinctive.

1. PHONOLITE - KENYTE SEQUENCE

Although about 3,000 metres of this succession is masked by later formations exposed mostly in the alpine zone, it is inferred from the fragments in the agglomerates that the bulk of the lavas of the main vent eruptions are phonolite-kenyte rocks. The presence of other types of lavas would most certainly be revealed by inclusions of their fragments in later lavas.

The phonolite-kenyte lavas and agglomerates on the mountain side, and the nepheline-syenite forming the plugs of the main and parasitic vents, are chemically alike, but show textural and grain size variations due to their differing rates of cooling.

The most important and abundant light-coloured minerals in these rocks are feldspars, commonly showing at least two generations of growth. The early ones are large, reaching two to four centimetres in size, and are tabular or elongated,

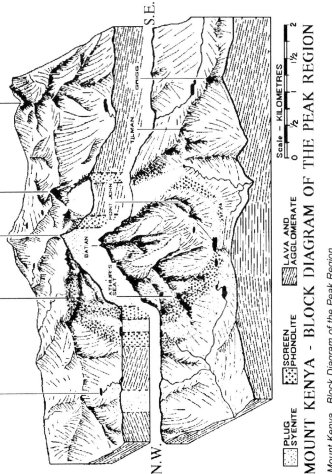

MOUNT KENYA - BLOCK DIAGRAM OF THE PEAK REGION

Mount Kenya. Block Diagram of the Peak Region.

Scale - KILOMETRES

0   ½   1   1½   2

PLUG SYENITE

SCREEN PHONOLITE

LAVA AND AGGLOMERATE

S.E.

N.W.

TILMAN

GRIGG

POINT JOHN

BATIAN

ATHER'S SEAT

57

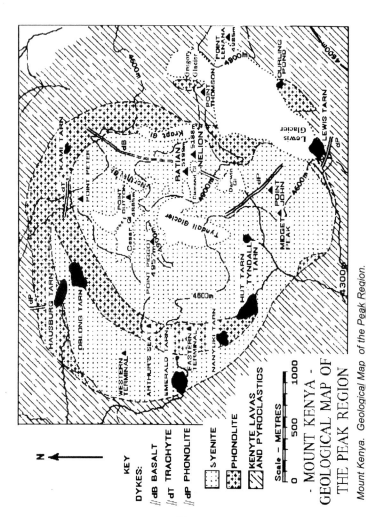

KEY

DYKES:
dB BASALT
dT TRACHYTE
dP PHONOLITE

SYENITE

PHONOLITE

KENYTE LAVAS
AND PYROCLASTICS

Scale – METRES
0   500   1000

- MOUNT KENYA -
GEOLOGICAL MAP OF
THE PEAK REGION

Mount Kenya. Geological Map of the Peak Region.

and if present in the lavas, give porphyritic texture. Commonly these feldspars are transparent or white, with a vitreous lustre when fresh, and show good cleavages. The later generation may be present in the groundmass as microscopic laths; frequently the groundmass may be glassy due to sudden chilling.

Nepheline, which may be as abundant as feldspar is one of the characteristic minerals of alkaline lavas. It occurs as pale yellow, pink or greenish-white phenocrysts, reaching up to two centimetres across, and having a waxy appearance. It is easily weathered, leaving an empty cavity of the crystal shape in the rock. This mineral also readily alters to zeolite, a mineral which typically fills the bubble cavities of many alkaline lavas.

Phonolite lava sheets with subordinate agglomerates outcrop mainly in the eastern and western slopes of the mountain. They are mantled by younger lava formations in the north and south. Only the bouldery remains of the lavas projecting from the soil can be seen, in the forest belt, but on the moorlands, columnar cliffs of lava and conspicuous crags of agglomerate are common.

These volcanics are mostly porphyritic with large crystal of feldspar and nepheline, set in a greenish-grey, fine-grained ground-mass. Zeolite fillings in bubble cavities are common.

About five kilometres from the central plug there is a transition from phonolites to kenytes, and the agglomerates become dominant over the lava sheets which are rather thin. The phenocryst constituents of feldspar and nepheline remain the same and the fresh ground-mass of kenyte is black, glassy and flow-banded. Later processes, including weathering, alter the rock greatly. The glassy matrix is frequently devitrified, the phenocrysts are discoloured and the rock as a whole is coloured bright earthy buff, orange-purple, or grey, and is frost-shattered to gravel size scree. Extensive outcrops occur at the heads of Hobley and Gorges valleys, and on the mountainsides above 4,200 metres, including the peaks of Sendeyo, Coryndon, McMillan, Delamere and Lenana.

2. THE NEPHELINE - SYENITE COMPLEX

The highest peaks of the mountain are carved out of he complex plug filling the main vent of the volcano. The plug is composed of phonolite and its plutonic equivalent, nepheline-syenite, and has been intruded by dykes of varied rock types. The inner cylindrical core of nepheline-syenite coincides roughly with the 4,600 metres contour, and forms the central peaks including Batian and Nelion. Surrounding this inner core are partially cylindrical, vertical wedges of phonolites.

The phonolites (e.g. those forming the small ridges immediately west of Austrian Hut), are similar to the ones forming flows on the mountain-sides, except that the groundmass is darker grey to black, and not quite glassy. The contact margin of the phonolites with the core syenite shows shattering, penetration and alteration by the inner body of syenite.

The main syenite body contains fragments of phonolites and is grey in colour. Its margins are chilled and of fine gained texture, but it becomes coarse grained and massive away from the margins. Large tabular feldspars are conspicuous and the groundmass is composed of a mosaic of feldspars and pink nepheline crystals with occasional dark minerals.

A system of radial and concentric fracture joints, geometrically related to the cylindrical shape of the plug, is dominant. These are joints closely spaced in the finer grained phonolites and widely spaced in the coarse massive syenite. The principal mode of erosion is removal of rock blocks along vertical columns controlled by these joints, and this has left upstanding scenic but precipitous pinnacles and peaks.

It is of interest to note that the near glassy groundmass of the phonolite wedges indicates rapid cooling and freezing of rock very near the surface, while the coarse grained syenites suggest a deeply buried, well insulated magma which cooled slowly. The close proximity of the two raises problems of their mode and order of emplacement.

ERUPTIONS FORM PARASITIC VENTS

Parts of Mount Kenya display rocks which differ in their mineral composition or in their structural relationships to the main vent eruptions.

1. *Rhomb porphyries*, the oldest among the Mount Kenya suite of rocks and characterised by large rhombic feldspars, outcrop in the western sector of the mountain between the Liki North and Teleki Valleys. These are eruptions from a vent lying south-west of Polish-man's Tarn, where a syenite plug four hundred metres in diameter is exposed.

Trachytes are lavas which are free from silica and silica-deficient minerals like nepheline. They are generally more viscous than phonolites and lighter in colour, ranging from pale-grey, greenish-grey, to reddish-grey, and characteristically show flow-banding often contorted, and fissility. Feldspars are abundant with subordinate dark minerals. The formation of these lavas show rough jagged profiles, in contrast to the smooth plainer sheets of the phonolites.

2. *Trachytes and phonolites*, together with agglomerates form Shipton's peak and the cliffs overlooking Lake Hohnel, and outcrop in Teleki Valley and Hausburg valley. Their dips suggests source vent near Kampi ya Farasi, some 4.25 km west of Batian.

3. *Fissile phonolites*, which have a reddish tinge and are flow-laminated, crop out in the moorlands on the ridges between the Ontulili and Liki North rivers, and in Hausburg and Mackinder Valleys.

4. *Olivine trachytes*, outcrop in moorlands between Kazita East and Sirimon Valleys. These generally are flow banded lavas of even finer grain. On weathering they form toothed crags and linear, wall-like outcrop.

Hall Tarns stock is an oval platform reaching 1.5 km

in length, and three of its sides form precipitous cliffs. It is formed from a lava lake of olivine trachyte, that pooled in a vent whose agglomerate walls have subsequently been removed by erosion. The lavas, which grade from trachytes to darker basalts and which occur in an area extending from Lake Ellis to Urumandi, probably erupted from this vent.

5. *Pantelleritic trachytes* are light-coloured and easily weather to white sand. These soft rocks form isolated small outcrops and dykes. On erosion, the dykes have formed Simba Col, Hausburg Col, and cols between the Sirimon and Liki North Valleys, and between the Hinde and Kazita West Valleys.

6. *Olivine basalts* occur in the moorlands between the Ontulili and Sirimon Valleys. Further isolated outcrops and flows can be seen Northeast of the Barrow, in the Hobley Valley, on ridges between the Teleki and Sagana valleys, and in lower part of the Mackinder, like North and Ontulili Valleys. These basalts rest on the weathered surfaces of earlier main vent eruptions.

ERUPTIONS FROM LATER PARASITIC VENTS

These vents and their eruptions date the main mountain formation and are in early stages of dissection. They form two distinctive groups, the trachytic and basaltic.

1. Mugi Hill, lying about 1.6 km east of Lake Ellis, is low feature about 100 metres high, and formed from kenyte- phonolite sheets domed up by an internal intrusion of lavas. It seems to lie partly on an explosion crater. Its upper surface is faulted and fractured.

2. On the north-eastern side of the mountain re six trachytic necks lying both inside and outside the National Park boundary. Ithanguni is the highest and was once covered by ice.

Of the other five, Rutundu and Giant's Billiard table

are well developed. They are all sub circular, elevated features whose upper surfaces are smooth, sometimes with central depressions. They are formed form trachytes and are collared by horizontal lavas, agglomerate and pyroclasts. These volcanics also mantle wide areas of the mountain in the Northeast.

3. Basaltic lavas and vents of recent origin related to the Nyambeni volcanic field mantle the northern and southern slopes of the mountain. Lava flows, many small cones, vents and craters, which are barely dissected by erosion, can be seen on the moorland. Some of the cones show an alignment along a north-east direction. These basaltic lavas some of which are blocky and slaggy, are generally dark in colour and show large crystals of feldspars and small bottle-green olivines.

References:
Baker, B.H. *Geology of Mount Kenya area.* Geological Survey of Kenya, Report 79,1967.
Baker, B.H;Mohr, P.A; and William's, L.A.J. *Geology of the Eastern Rift System of Africa.* The Geological Society of America. Special Paper 136. 1972.

ACCESS TO MOUNT KENYA AREA

Entry

Visitors approaching the mountain from a route other than the three main routes (Naro Moru, Sirimon, or Chogoria) must inform the park warden beforehand.

Environment

Do not burn any vegetation, particularly dead Lobelias and Groundsels at the higher altitudes, which form an important part of the mountain's fragile ecosystem. There have been several huge fires in recent years over both higher and lower slopes. **Carry out all your litter.**

The majority of visitors Mount Kenya will pass through Nairobi, Kenya's capital city and chief shopping centre. Most supplies needed for the mountain can be purchased here, although it should be noted that dehydrated foods are difficult to obtain. Visitors from overseas would do well to bring a supply of freeze dried food with them.

Nairobi has many hotels, catering for all pockets, and a wide selection of different restaurants. Lists of hotels and restaurants can be found in most general tourist handbooks.

Nairobi abounds with car-hire firms, dealing in self-drive and chauffeur-driven cars and four-wheel drive vehicles. A list of these businesses can be found in the yellow pages of the Kenya Telephone Directory. A hired car is obviously the most convenient way of reaching Mount Kenya.

The main centres at the foot of Mount Kenya from where the routes to the peaks begin are: Naro Moru (171 km. from Nairobi); Nanyuki (200 km from Nairobi); Meru (290 km. from Nairobi); Chogoria (228 km. from Nairobi); and Embu (142 km. from Nairobi).

There is a good bus service daily linking Nairobi with Naro Moru, Nanyuki, Chogoria and Meru. Contact:

Akamba Public Road Services
Lagos Road
P.O BOX 40322
Nairobi Phone 340430

For transportation to the east side of the mountain, contact:

Kensilver Express
P.O Box 34003
Nairobi Phone 221839

Mini buses and road taxis for both Nanyuki and Meru leave from Accra Road. No bookings needed.

It is possible to find camping sites at the base of Mount Kenya, and most towns in the region possess small camping areas. Many hotels offer camping facilities, but climbers would do well to make for National Park Gate or Forest Station entrances, where campers are welcome.

TRANSPORT ON THE MOUNTAIN

From roadheads' on the various mountain tracks, parties must either carry their own loads for the first day or two to the peak area, or hire porters. For those unacquainted with the higher altitudes, porters are a worthy consideration.

The Naro Moru, Sirimon and Chogoria Tracks are being maintained to a standard which except in very wet weather, will allow private cars with drivers suitably experienced in driving on dirt tracks to reach approximately 3,000 metres. Four-wheel drive vehicles will reach this altitude even when it is fairly wet and on the Sirimon Track 3,300 metres.

Guides and Porters

Porters are becoming increasingly used on Mount Kenya. Porters, cooks, and guides are now registered by the National Park or the Association of Mount Kenya Operators (AMKO), and issued with an identity card including a photograph of the holder. Only those who are registered should be employed; note the name and number before setting out so that any complaint made in writing to the Park Authorities can be effectively followed up. Visitors should pay for their park fees and obtain all receipts for the park, which must be shown when leaving.

Current rates of pay are around US $ 6.00 a day for a porter, a little more for a guide or cook. These prices are subject to change without notice. Porters and guides should provide their own food, clothing and equipment. The employer provides the rucksack, the weight of which is included in the load of 18 kg.

Many porters are willing and able to carry more if increased pay is offered. Establish beforehand what constitutes a day's work. On a long trip make sure your porters have enough food with them. Porters expect to have transport provided for their descent. Porters are responsible only for load-carrying, and should not be expected to guide parties on walking routes, nor do ascents of even minor peaks, as for example, Point Lenana. Guides will advise on, and carry out, ascents of Point Lenana, but are not generally suitable for any other climbs. Note that Mount Kenya porters (unlike those on Kilimanjaro), do not carry loads on their heads.

On a day when porters carry loads up to a high hut, time must be allowed for them to descend to a camp-site in a valley head.

For visitors requiring porters on the Naro Moru Track and the Sirimon Track, contact:

The Naro Moru Porters and Guides Association
Phone: 0176 - 62015

Note that for the Sirimon track, clients must arrange transport for the porters from Naro Moru.

For the Sirimon Track, porters are also available through:

Bantu Utamaduni Lodge
P.O Box 333
Nanyuki
Phone: 0176 - 62625

For Chogoria Route porters, visitors should contact:
Mt. Kenya Transverser
P.O Box 83
Chogoria

The services porters render can make or spoil a visit to Mount Kenya. Local climbers tend to make little use of them. It is therefore important that visitors should handle their porter situation with care, and follow the advice given above.

MAPS OF MOUNT KENYA

At the present time there is only one map available which adequately covers the Mount Kenya area. It is drawn and published by M. Savage and A. Wielochowski and is at 1:50,000 scale.

Maps published by the Survey of Kenya at 1:125,000 and 1:25,000 are also available from time to time, but are often out of print.

MOUNT KENYA NATIONAL PARK PROCEDURE

Entry: Park fees as of August 1998 (payable in US$, or KSh equivalent):
Adults (non residents) US$ 15 per day, (residents) KSh 100.
Climbers (non residents) US$ 10 per day.
Students, children (under 18) & organised groups (given prior notice to Park Warden) US$ 5 per day.
camping (non residents) US$ 2 per night, (residents) KSh 50.

The Mount Kenya National Park consist of all ground above 10,500 feet, and salients running astride the Naro Moru and Sirimon Tracks respectively. It is administered by:

The Warden
Mount kenya National Park
P.O Box 69
Naro Moru

The Warden lives at the Park Headquarters which is located at the Naro Moru Park Gate.

The remainder of the mountain is Forest reserve administered by the Divisional Forest Officer, P.O. BOX 28 Nyeri.

Permission is required to enter the National Park and may be obtained by signing in, and paying fees at Park entrance Gates. Park fees are subject to change without notice.

Visitors staying in the Park overnight are obliged to pay camping fees, unless they are in possession of a valid booking voucher.

ACCIDENT PROCEDURE

The mountain forest, in particular, are the natural habitat of elephant, buffalo, rhinoceros, and other large game. These should be considered a potential source of danger, and care should be taken when using forest tracks to the moorlands. It is most inadvisable to travel on foot through the forest at night; the results have been fatal. If in an emergency a night journey is unavoidable, it is generally considered best to move noisily through the forest. Most animals will move off if given such warning of approach.

The National Park has established a permanently manned ranger Station at the head of the Teleki Valley. This Station possesses oxygen and the medical supplies necessary for an evacuation. The rangers who live at the Station, are well qualified in Mountain Rescue techniques, and are in radio contacted with Park Headquarters.

If an accident or illness should occur in the peak area the following steps should be taken:
1. Make sure that nor further damage threaten either the patient or the remainder of the party.
2. Carry out any immediate first aid necessary, and reassure all members of the party (Consult the Mountain Medicine Section in this book).
3. Send a message for help to the Ranger Station in the Teleki Valley.
The messenger(s), should possess the following information:
(a) Place of accident with detailed map reference, or name of

climb, and position on climb where accident or illness occurred.

(b) Time of accident or illness

(c) Nature of injuries or illness.

(d) Name, age and sex of injured person(s).

The messenger should preferably go with a companion, and both should carry a written note with all the above details listed. Verbal messages are inadequate and invariably lead to confusion. If porters are used as messengers, they should be sent unladen, and instructed to show the message to any other parties they might see. They should be promised a substantial tip if they deliver the message quickly.

In case help may be within earshot, the internationally recognised mountain alarm signal consists of six long whistle-blasts or torch-flashes, spread over a period of a minute, then a pause of a minute, followed by the signal repeated, etc. The reply to acknowledge this signal consists of three long blasts-flashes in a minute. In the event of an accident everyone at hand is expected to help even if it means abandoning some long-planned project.

Someone should remain with the patient, erect a shelter of some sort, keep them warm, administer first aid give them food and drink a far as there injuries allow, and comfort them.

If it is unavoidable that the patient has to be left alone in the shelter which has been erected, they must be told to stay put at all costs, and food, water, and spare clothing be left with them. A torch (flashlight), an whistle should also be left if possible. An unconscious patient should not be left alone, but if this is unavoidable and they are injured on a climb, he should be secured to the surrounding rocks. The spot where the patient lies should be marked as conspicuously as possible.

Climbers who get lost on the mountain should stick together and stay on the moorlands rather than in the forest. If completely lost it is usually better to stay put, rather than wander about aimlessly, and to wait for the weather to clear. Pick some shelter (especially from the wind), and collect fuel before it gets dark. Fires should be lit to attract the attention of searchers, but take care not to start a moorland fire. The leader of the group must watch less experienced members very closely. All in the party should possess, carry, and be able to use a map and compass.

They should watch and listen for the searching aircraft (probably in the clear weather period in the morning), and wave some large brightly coloured garment until they have been seen. They must remain where they are until rangers arrive.

If the party is lost in the forest, remember that ridges are easier going than valleys. Try not to be misled by game trails; buffaloes have cloven hooves.

HUTS ON MOUNT KENYA

Minto's hut on the Chogoria route is now for porters' use only. The Chogoria Route is only for parties equipped for camping. Tents must be shown at the Chogoria Park Gate before parties are allowed access.

Baillie's Bivi and Urumandi Hut are almost unusable.

The largest high altitude hut on the mountain is the Teleki Valley Lodge owned and run by Naro Moru River Lodge. It costs Kshs 500.00 per person per night and can be booked through Naro Moru River Lodge, P.O Box 18, Phone: Nanyuki 0176 - 62622 or Alliance Hotels, P.O Box 49839, Nairobi: Phone 337501. Bantu Lodge operate structures above the campsite at the end of the access road to the Sirimon Route and Shipton's Cave in the Mackinder valley. Arrangements to use should be made through Bantu Utamanduni Lodge, P.O. Box 333 Nanyuki - Phone: 0176 - 62625

The remaining high altitude huts (except the National Park Rangers station in Teleki Valley), were built and used to be the property of the Mountain Club of Kenya. Ownership and management of these huts may be changed to the National Park. For the latest information on the availability and booking procedures to members of the M.C.K. and non members, please contact the Warden of the National Park or the Mountain Club of Kenya.

Hut bookings once paid for are acknowledged by means of a hut booking voucher, which must be produced at the Mount Kenya National Park gate on entry.

Top Hut (located beside Austrian Hut) and the two locked Rescue Huts at Kami and in the Teleki valley, are reserved for the sole use of the M.C.K. and it is illegal for non-members to make use of them.

PARTIES USING THESE HUTS SHOULD LEAVE THEM CLEAN AND TIDY, AND BRING ALL GARBAGE OFF THE MOUNTAIN. PLEASE DO NOT MAKE USE OF OLD RUBBISH DUMPS.

1. Top Hut (4,790 m), is situated on the east side of the Lewis Glacier and is conveniently located for parties attempting the Normal Route up Batian. Water is available from the Curling Pond or nearby puddles. The original wooden hut was built by Ernest Carr about 1925; it was blown down shortly after but later reconstructed. It is now reserved for members of the M.C.K.

2. Austrian Hut (4,790 m), has three rooms and sleeps 30 people. It was opened in February 1973 an completed and in use well under one year from the time of the destruction of its forerunner - the Authur Firmin Memorial Hut. It is located next to the old Top Hut, and was erected by John (Minto) Nuttall and Tim Andersen, much of the funds being contributed by Mr. Marcus Schmuck and his Austrian colleagues.

3. Two Tarn Hut (4,490 m), was erected by the Mountain Club of Kenya in 1948 beside the upper lake on Two Tarn col. It is one-roomed structure containing shelf-type accommodation. Beautifully situated, it is an ideal starting point for routes on the southern and western sides of Batian.

4. Kami Hut (4,439 m), was constructed in January 1963, much of the material having been damaged in a rather unsuccessful air-drop. In 1986 it was rebuilt 100 m away from its former site by Kami Tarn which had become rather polluted. It forms an excellent base for North Face climbers, as well as being a convenient place for round-the-peak walkers to break their journey. It is of aluminium, and provides basic shelter for eight people. It stands next to the Kami Rescue Hut.

5. Liki North Hut (3,993 m), is the only hut situated on the north-western moorlands, and was erected in 1970. It can sleep about eight persons. The hut is an excellent base for climbs on Tereri and Sendeyo, and also forms a convenient overnight stop between the top of the Sirimon Track, and Kami, Hall tarns or Austrian Hut.

6. Minto's Hut (4,297 m), is on the east side of the mountain by the Gorges Valley. The main force behind the building of this hut was John (Minto) Nuttall, and it was erected in 1966. It is a splendidly sited hut by Hall Tarns with a sleeping shelf for 8 persons. In 1988 it was relocated away from the tarn and refurbished by Operation Raleigh.

7. Urumandi Hut (3,063 m), was built in 1923 by Ernest Carr on the Chogoria Route. It is situated in a well sheltered spot in the giant heath and parkland zone. It is a wooden structure without furniture. Water is available nearby down a steep slope.

8. Baillie's Bivvy (5,000 m), is a bivouac shelter located at Mackinder's Gendarme on the South-east Face of Nelion. It was erected by Rusty Baillie in the early 1960s and contains no equipment. For much of the year, the floor and part of the space remains iced-up, and the door is missing.

9. Howell Hut (5,188 m), This magnificent bivouac shelter is located on the summit of Nelion. It was built by Ian Howell in February 1970 after five loads had been successfully parachuted onto the Lewis Glacier. In a feat which can only be described as remarkable, Howell then made thirteen solo ascent of Nelion as he gradually carried the materials to the summit. The floor is foam covered.

The Teleki Hut and Klarwills Hut have both now been demolished.

In addition to the high altitude huts there is self-service accommodation at or near the roadhead on the Naro Moru Track and the Chogoria track. The Met Station Bandas (also known as Meru Mt. Kenya Lodge) on the Naro Moru Track are booked through Naro Moru River Lodge, and the Chogoria Bandas on the Chogoria Track can be booked through travel agents in Nairobi.

FOREST AND MOORLANDS ROUTES
ON MOUNT KENYA

The principal obstacle to reaching the higher regions of Mount Kenya is the forest, which in most parts is so dense that only cleared tracks are practicable. The routes are here described in clockwise order round the mountain.

Timings given should be adequate for moderately fit parties not too heavily laden, with allowance only for brief halts. A good reserve should always be allowed for, and a start should be made early in the morning. For the descent allow at least half the time taken on the ascent.

1. NARO MORU TRACK

This route to the Teleki Valley is the shortest way to the peaks, and is one of the most popular track at the present time. Owing to the fact that it is the shortest way up the mountain, there is a tendency for visitors to ascend too quickly and become the victims of Mountain Sickness and other illnesses related to altitude. It is therefore strongly advised that visitors unaccustomed to high altitude should consider hiking the first day from the Park Gate to the Meteorological Clearing, rather than make use of a vehicle for this important stage of the ascent. Please refer to section of Mountain Medicine.

From opposite Naro Moru Police Station a well sign-posted road leads in 17 km. to the Mount Kenya National Park entrance. A further 9 km. of good track leads past Percival's Bridge to the Meteorological Clearing at 3,050 m. Only official vehicles may drive above this point. Campsites, self-service lodge facilities, and water are available at this location. The track climbs more steeply, passes the Police Signals Station, then narrows to a footpath leading to the edge of the forest. From the Meteorological Clearing to this point takes about one hour.

A steep, marshy section known as the 'vertical bog" follows. The route keeps to the south side of the ridge, through open moorland until (about 3 1/2 to 4 hours from the Met. Clearing), the path reaches the crest of the ridge overlooking Teleki valley (4,000 m). The path contours along the south side of the Teleki Valley, keeping first high, and then gradually descends to reach the valley floor. It then follows the valley to reach the Mackinder's Camp. From the Met. Clearing to here is about five to six hours.

The Austrian Hut can be reached in a further three or four hours, but it is advisable not to attempt this from the Met. Clearing the same day. Two paths lead to Austrian Hut. The old path (and the one likely to be used by people camping at the head of Teleki Valley), leads up the valley then climbs the scree to the north of Shipton's Peak. A recently developed path leads from the lodge and contours up the left-hand side of Teleki Valley to join the original path at the stream northwest of Shipton's Peak. A long pull then leads up the lateral moraine of the Lewis Glacier, veering left to the rocky bluff where the Austrian Hut is situated.

The ranger Station is located near the head of the Teleki Valley. Two Tarn Hut is best reached by mounting the white scree behind the Ranger Station and climbing diagonally up the side of the valley to Hut Tarn (1 1/2 hours).

2. BURGURET ROUTE

This track is almost never used nowadays but in the past was a popular mule-trail. It leads to Two Tarn Col, and is really only suitable for the January-March season. There used to be an old mule route from Kangaiti Rifle Range (near Nanyuki), up the ridge between the Ontulili and Liki North Valleys then bearing right on the moorlands across the ridge to the Mackinder valley, but it has not been used for many years.

Roadhead for the Burguret Route is at the Game Department but mules are loaded either at May's Farm or at the Gathiuru Forest Station a mile before reaching the Game Department. Some people prefer to walk up from the farm to the Forest Station to help acclimatise to the altitude. To reach the Forest Station take the track which leaves the main road 9 km. south of Nanyuki; the Forest Station is 11 km. up this track, and cars may be left here by arrangement with the Forest Officer.

After passing the Game Department (which may not be occupied), the track forks right through forestry plantations and soon passes through a game fence into the forest proper; this consists at first mainly of cedar, but very soon bamboo takes over and continues for many kilometres, cutting out all views.

The track follows a ridge, the gradient at first being quite gentle, but there are some steeper section later. About 4 1/2 hours from the Game Department a small clearing is reached - Kampi ya Machengeni (2,990 m), - with a small stream close by. This is a good compact campsite.

The gradient now steepens and the track zigzags. After 3/4 hour a belt of giant heath is reached at the top of the forest, and another 3/4 hour brings one to Kampi ya K.A.R. (3,500 m), situated beside large rocks on a ridge between the deep Nanyuki South Valley and a shallower Burguret tributary valley (where water is normally available). The track continues up the ridge for a short time and then veers right through tussock grass to cross a small ridge and enter the Buguret Valley on its true right bank. The track now descends slightly to pass below the bluffs of Highland castle, where there are caves suitable for sleeping in and then cross the Burguret River to its left bank. There are several possible campsites in this section. These campsites may be marshy in a wet season, especially Kampi ya Farasi.

Near the head of the valley a precipice comes into view. To avoid it the track swing left from Kampi ya Farasi (about four hours from Kampi ya K.A.R., 5 1/2 km. from Kampi ya Machengeni), and climbs steeply out of the valley. Then on the ridge it bears right again, and fairly easy walking over rocky ground brings one round the back of a hill (4,538 m), and then swings left to two Tarn Hut 4,490 m). The route is well cairned.

From Kampi ya K.A.R. to Two Tarn Hut is 5½ to 6 hours' walk.

From Two tarn Hut it is possible to reach Austrian Hut in 2½ to 3 hours, the old mule route going down to the broad shelf above the head of the main Teleki Valley before starting the ascent up the moraine to Austrian Hut.

Bantu Lodge have developed three new routes which follow roughly similar lines to the old Burguret Route. It is essential to take a guide from the Lodge for these.

3. SIRIMON TRACK

This track provides the easiest access to the northern side of the central peaks, and the quickest way to Liki North and Kami huts. It is a beautiful route with fine view of Sendeyo and Tereri, and of the main peaks.

15 km. from Nanyuki on the Timau road, just before the road winds down to cross the Sirimon River, a signposted track turns S.E., and leads in 10 km. to the National Park gate. 3 km. past the gate at about 2,900 m, a series of a steep gradients begins, but most cars can continue a further 5 km. in the dry season, to a good campsite at 3,350 m, where a stream crosses the track. Four-wheel drive vehicles can go a little further.

The track continues from the campsite over the moorlands, past the 12,000 ft. rain-gauge, and peters out at about 4,000 m below a prominent hill called The Barrow, 4,195 m. Vehicles could once reach the 13,500 ft. rain-gauge.

From the Sirimon Track there are several possible routes:
a)To the Mackinder Valley and Kami Hut either direct or via the Liki North Hut and b) to Austrian Hut or Hall tarns Hut, either via the Liki North Hut, or by the former mule track over the col at the head of the Kazita West Valley.

For the Liki North Hut and the Mackinder Valley leave a track about 1 km. after passing the 12,000 ft. rain-gauge, and make a lightly rising traverse to the south to cross the Ontulili stream and the valley, and follow the stream up to

Mount Kenya. Top Hut (left) and Austrian Hut.

David Keith Jones

the Liki North Hut situated at 3,993 m, about four hours walk from the 3,300 m campsite.

To go on to Kami Hut it is not necessary to follow the stream up to Liki North Hut, but instead the Liki North valley should be crossed, and the major ridge beyond crossed to drop down into the Mackinder valley. A clearly defined track eventually crosses the main Liki stream to reach a good camp-site below some obvious rock there in a further 1 1/2 - 2 hours by mounting diagonally up the steep valley side in the direction of the main peaks. Part of this section is cairned. Alternatively, from Shipton's Cave, carry on up the Mackinder valley for 1/2 - 1 hour to reach Bantu Lodge's structures.

The Mackinder Valley and Kami Hut can also be reached in a long day's walk from the 3,300 m campsite by crossing both the Ontulili and Liki North Valleys, and instead of turning up towards the Liki North Hut aim for a cairned platform at 4,180 m on the ridge overlooking the Valley - 4 1/2 hours from campsite. The descent into past Shaitani, and other caves suitable for bivouacs, is awkward; the route then follows the contour path on the eastern side of the valley to join the route from the Liki North Hut described above, to reach Shipton's Cave in about 7 hours from the campsite.

To go from Liki North Hut to Austrian Hut or Hall Tarns Hut, continue up the Liki North Valley to the cliff-sided ridge running Northeast from Sendeyo above the head of the Sirimon Valley, and find a gap through the cliffs into the head of the Hinde Valley (At the head of the Hinde Valley South of this gap at about 4,500 m lies the skeleton of an elephant). To reach Austrian Hut swing south and follow the rocky ridge round the heads of both branches of the Hinde Valley to Simba Col and thence to Square Tarn, where the route from Hall Tarns to Austrian Hut is joined. The traverse over Lenana from Simba Col is a mild rock or snow climb and is not a porter route.

For Minto's Hut drop into the Hinde valley from the gap in the Northeast ridge of Sendeyo and join the mule track

which comes over the col from the Kazita west valley. Follow
this track until it turns into the south-west branch of the Hinde
Valley, at which point leave it and cross the entrance of the
branch valley and carry on down the south side of the main
Hinde Valley, rising gently towards a col behind a rounded spur
that juts out of the valley side. Shortly before the col turn south
and follow a gully that leads over the ridge form which the various Hall Tarns can be seen. An easy scree slope leads down
to the tarns and Minto's Hut at 4,297 m.

A proven route for mules from the Sirimon track to
Austrian Hut - a two day journey - is to follow the Sirimon Track
until about 3,650 m and then traverse left into a valley, near the
head of which go east over a col (4,163 m), into the main
Sirimon Valley. The Sirimon stream is crossed, and again the
route goes east to climb out of a valley between a large tooth
of rock on the left and a long line of precipices on the right.
Now keeping high, work right-handed to find a high col at the
head of the Kazita West Valley; this col gives access to the
Hinde Valley, where there are several good campsites (8 hours
from 3,300 m. campsite). From the south-western head of the
Hinde Valley there is a climb (hard for mules) to a col overlooking the valley, and from here Simba Col may be reached and
the route from Hall Tarns to Austrian Hut joined at Square Tarn.

4. TIMAU TRACK

This track has not been used for some time and
those wishing to ascend it would be advised to contact the
National Park Warden for up-to-date information. It used to be
the highest point one could reach on the mountain in a vehicle
- approximately 4,190 m, although it is now no longer worth driving above 3,380 m as progress is slow.

From Nanyuki take the Timau road for 19 km., and
turn right onto a farm track which may be signboarded "Timau
Settlement Officer's House". Veer left at a farmhouse after 3
km. and right at a "T" junction 5 km. from the Timau road.
Continue through the settlement farms - farm tracks liable to

change - and cross the Mount Kenya Forest Boundary (notice board), about 7 km. from the main road. At 8 km. take the left fork and cross two bridges within the next 11/2 km. The track now turns generally easterly past a Ranger's Post at 14 km. and then north to a junction at 26 km. Turn South - hard right and follow the main track, crossing the Kisima Track at 29 km., and passing a fire fighters hut (Wilson's Hut) in 3 km. The track continues over moorlands for a further 14 km. to cross the Kazita West river at 48 km., and ends 52 km. from the main road. (Ref. on 1:25,000 map is 43 mm. east of Long. 37⁰20', 80 mm. south of Lat. 0⁰5'26").

From the old roadhead Minto's Hut can be reached in 3-4 hours and Top Hut via Simba Col in a long day. For both routes go round the hill blocking past a ridge ahead on the east side (it pays to go down and round and not to mind losing some height), and go south-westerly to the high col at the head of the Kazita West Valley leading to the Hinde Valley. The mule track from the head of the Sirimon Track can be joined before the end. From the south-western head of the Hinde Valley there is a climb to a col overlooking the MackinderValley, and from here Simba Col may be reached and the route from Hall tarns to Top Hut joined at Square Tarn.

5. MERU ROUTE

There has been much forest cutting in the vicinity of this little used route in recent years, and the following descrip-tion should be followed with caution. Prior to this forest destruction the route provided an easy two to three hours' walk from roadhead to Lake Rutundu, and an interesting two to three days' walk into the peak area.

From Meru, go to Katheri. Pass Katheri Market, and after about 500 metres across a bridge with guard rail, and immediately fork right. After another 500 metres there is a pos-sible left turn into some buildings, but ignore this turn. Turn left after another 500 metres; this is a right-angle turn between two hedge. A further 500 metres on, cross a bridge over a small stream, and after a similar distance turn right at small shop on the right. The track goes round a right-angle to the left, followed almost immediately by another to the right, within few hundred metres of the junction.

After 7 km. the end of the small farm plots is reached, and the beginning of the Forest Reserve starts. After about 1.5 km. a series of hairpin bends starts, and the track deteriorates and becomes impassable for ordinary cars within the next 500 metres or so even when dry.

The edge of the clearing is 2 km. further on, and the campsite at the far side of the clearing is about 1,000 metres away. The campsite is a river, with a disused forestry hut on the left. From here there are fine walks to Ithanguni and Lakes Alice and Rutundu.

6. CHOGORIA ROUTE

This route begins from Chogoria, a Church of Scotland Mission Station to the east of the mountain, about 96 km. from Embu and 64 km. from Meru. This route, regarded by many people as the most beautiful on the mountain, was opened up in the 1920s by Earnest Carr, who made a vehicle track to the moorlands, and it was for many years the most popular route to the peaks. It is a long route, and parties wanting porters should contact Mr. Livingstone Barine, P.O. Box 5007, Chogoria. Telephone Chogoria 26.

In recent years much development has taken place in the lower forest and bamboo zones, and Meru Country Council has been responsible for renovating the road as far as the park-like "Urumandi Glade" country at 3,000 m. Although this has resulted in easier access for visitors even in ordinary cars, it has virtually ruined the unique atmosphere of the lower giant camphor forest. Gone are the days when the hiker could spend half a day tunnelling through the bamboo - there is now a wide easily motorable road through this area. If there is one positive element it is that the moorland area of Lake Ellis, Mugi Hill and Kilingo (Giant's Billiard Table), is easier to reach; this is

Mount Kenya. Main Peaks seen from Hall Tarns on the Chogoria Route.

David Keith Jones

some of the finest hiking country on Mount Kenya and the visitor should be aware of this.

4 km. from Chogoria, accessible by public transport is Mutindua, a small market with several houses, and shortly past this village is the Forestry Department Station and gate. There is a good campsite at the Station. People walking form this point will make for Bairunyi Clearing (2,700 m) on the first day, which is 16 km. from the Forest Station. Water should be carried this day as it is not easy to find on the walk, (porters will know of a spot about halfway). Water is available down the steep slope of the valley south of the camp, where there is a river. If the track is dry and in good condition ordinary cars can reach the self-service Meru Mount Kenya Lodge (Chogoria Bandas) at 3,000 m. 4 WD vehicles can follow a rough track 6 km. further up the mountain. The park gate is just below the bandas. There is a campsite nearby and suitable spots at the roadhead. If you drive to the roadhead you should pay track fees, collected at the bandas for Meru County Council.

From the roadhead, the route to Hall Tarns crosses the stream and goes up the side of the ridge where the final thirteen zigzags of Carr's Motor Road can be seen on the right, petering out at 3,700 m. The route leads up the northeastern side of the Nithi Gorge and reaches Minto's Hut in about 6 hours.

Minto's Hut (4,300 m), is an excellently sited hut by Hall Tarns on the plateau overlooking Lake Michaelson (300 m below). Visitors would do well to take special note of the spectacular views of the Nithi Gorge, by walking ten minutes southeast of the hut to the edge of "The Temple".

From Hall Tarns the track continues to Austrian Hut (31/2 hours) via Square Tarn and The Tooth, then round the head of the Hobley Valley. Alternatively Kami Hut may be reached (3 hours) by crossing the lateral moraine of the Gregory Glacier to avoid losing too much height.

Further details of "Carr's Road" are given in M.C.K. Bulletins Nos. 46 and 47 (1958-59).

7. KAMWETI TRACK

This very little-used route provide access to the peaks via the southern moorlands. Two days are required for the walk from Kamweti Forest Station at 2,500 m to Austrian Hut.

To reach Kamweti, drive to Kutus village on the Sagana-Embu road. At the turning point 0.5 km. east of the village, take the tarmac road signposted to Kianyaga, but after 2 km. bear left onto a good dirt road which passes Kabare and Mutige Schools and 20 km. from Kutus enters the forest at Thiba Fishing Camp, where rondavels may be hired. The forestry track is motorable in dry weather, but logging trucks may render it impassable even for four-wheel drive vehicles after rain. 6 km. beyond Thiba is Castle Forest Station; a large two-storey house standing in a clearing in the forest. After Castle, the track continues a further 7 km. to Kamweti Forest Station, which is 145 km. from Nairobi. Cars may safely be left here and water is available.

From Kamweti, a track dating from the Emergency, leads up through bamboo to the 10,000 ft. raingauge. This is no longer motorable, and the walk takes two hours. No visible tracks exists above 3,000 m. From the raingauge, move due north through undulating bamboo, dense in places, and giant heather, keeping to the right of the prominent bamboo-covered hill. After 1 1/2 hours the forest is exited on the ridge. An hour after the end of the forest, the head of the Kiringa, known as The Bowl, is passed on the left. From this point the tussock grass makes for hard going, and to minimise this it is imperative to keep at least 1 km to the west of the Nyamindi West, even though this involves a slight detour to the left. 2 1/2 hours beyond The Bowl, turn N.N.E. and cross the Nyamindi West heading for an obvious scree slope, to the N.W. of some prominent crags (spot height 13,599 ft. on the 1:50,000 map). Below the scree is the Scoop, a good half-way camping place with plenty of water. From the Scoop, proceed directly up the scree to attain a stony ridge-top. Move along the ridge for 1 1/2 km.

Mount. Kenya. Climbing the Diamond Couloir.   *Ian Howell*

The going here is easy, a pleasant airy respite! Rather than following the ridge up to an unnamed peak overlooking Teleki Valley, contour right above Hidden Tarn and ascend scree slope, the top of which is close to Sommerfelt Peak. Now descend a few hundred feet and contour round the head of Teleki Valley just below and to the west of Grigg and Tilman Peaks. The ground is steep and boulder-covered, and the going slow and strenuous. Join the ridge to the north of Tilman Peak and continue to Austrian Hut.

From a camp in the Scoop it is possible to reach Lake Hohnel and Castle Hill by continuing up the Nyamindi West, or Hobley Valley by crossing to the east of the Nyamindi River. Details of these variations may be found in the Bulletin of the M.C.K. number 66, June 1968.

Another way by which the southern moorlands could be reached in the past was the "Gunia" Track. This track, which could be reached either from Karatina or from Kiganjo was constructed by the Royal Engineers during the Emergency and it followed a ridge to the south of the Sagana valley as far as the top of the forest. But the track has not been maintained and is unfit for any kind of vehicle after 21/2 km. from roadhead it is two days walk to Teleki Valley.

There is another route through the forest, from the region of Mountain Lodge, but it is as yet unofficial, and special permission should be granted by the Mount Kenya National Park Warden. For a description of the route see Mountain Club of Kenya Bulletin No. 72, 1974.

CLIMBING SEASONS ON MOUNT KENYA

Storms: Although storms on Mount Kenya do not match the level of those which frequent most other high peaks of the world, there has been a marked change in the severity of storms, particularly around August and September.

Rockfalls: With less rocks being held on, or in glaciers, there has been an increasing incidents of rockfalls on climbing routes.

Climbing conditions on Mount Kenya depend on the state of the rainy season, and the position of the sun. The old established dry periods are Christmas to mid-March and July to October, and these were considered reliable. In recent years snow storms of sufficient intensity to "write-off" rock climbs for several days have been quite common throughout the year. Ice routes are less affected by snow storms. It is difficult to say whether the reliable seasons will return. Assuming the weather is favourable at the times stated, different routes are in condition at different times.

Generally the south side of the mountain is in its summer condition from Christmas to mid-March, and in is winter condition from June to October. The north side follows the reverse pattern. Therefore, south facing rock routes such as the Normal Route on Nelion, Southern Slabs Route, the climbs on the Diamond Buttress and the South-West Ridge Route, are best enjoyed from Christmas to mid-March.

In late March the sun passes its zenith, and south facing rock begins to ice-up. The Diamond Couloir and the Ice Window Route have their full winter mantle from June to October, and these months are considered to be the best and safest times for climbing them. It is something of a paradox that the Diamond Couloir and its "Headwall" have received more ascents during the Christmas to mid-March season. January is sometimes so dry that the lower crux ice-fall on the Diamond Couloir turns into a rock climb!

The climbs on Mount Kenya's eastern side have to be considered differently. Owing to the sun being more prevalent in the morning than any other time of day, rock climbs facing east, irrespective of where they are situated on the mountain, tend to be free of ice during the two climbing seasons. The East Face Route on Nelion and the Northern Slabs Route on Batian fall in this category, although Northern Slabs was thought to be safer in the January-February season when the adjacent North Gate Route "Supercouloir" is iced up. The Eastern Groove Route, Scott-Braithwaite Route are, however, in condition during the June to October season, while the North-East Buttress of Batian should be climbed in January and February. This is because the big diedre, which is one of the main features on the lower section of this route, faces south.

The west side of the mountain receives less sun than east and it takes longer to clear after a fall of snow.

This will be noticed in the upper amphitheatre of the South-West Ridge Route on Batian. The West Ridge is a "mixed" route in either season but is probably easier when the North Face is clear of snow.

CLIMBING ON MOUNT KENYA

There is plenty of excellent ridge walking and scrambling up to heights of over 4,600 m on Mount Kenya. But with the exception of Point Lenana, there are no simple routes up any of the central peaks.

Point Lenana

With recent warming and recession of the glaciers on Mt. Kenya, the Lewis Glacier now often has a hard snow or ice cover, making walking over it hazardous without the proper equipment (crampons, ice axe).

Since the 1990 edition of the Guide to Mount Kenya and Kilimanjaro, changes in the environment around both mountains are having an effect on certain climbs.

The routes mentioned below should only be attempted by experienced climbers. For Climbing Standards attention is drawn to the section of this title in Part One of this book.

Descent of Nelion

There is now a bolted abseil route off Nelion, close to the Normal Route. Originally to facilitate rescues, this descent route is also recommended for climbers. The bolts have been placed close enough for single rope abseils. The descent tries to avoid the Normal Route ascent and is marked in places with paint arrows. Care must still be taken to ensure not to get off route, particularly to avoid descending to far into the south face, or too far to the north of Baillie's Bivi. During the winter season (July, August, September), ice can cover some of the bolts. There is still a lot of loose rock in places.

Gate of the Mists

From Christmas to March, climbers should be aware of the increasing difficulties in traversing the Gate of the Mists. Parties doing the Normal Route should now make crampons and ice axes a mandatory part of their equipment for traversing the Lewis Glacier and the Gate of the Mists. Obviously this situation is tough on those climbing the harder South Face routes: who wants to carry ice gear up the Diamond Buttress routes? Currently there is not a good, solid, safe descent route down Batian itself.

INDEX TO CLIMBING ROUTES ON
MOUNT KENYA

The following are routes. All the routes on Batian and Nelion should be regarded as 2 day climbs.

ROUTES ON BATIAN (5,199 M)
and
NELION (5,,188 M)

Route	Standard	Starting Hut	Time
1. Normal	V inf.	Austrian Hut	7 hrs
2. Mackinder's	IV.	Austrian Hut	7 hrs
3. South face	IV.	Two Tarn	8 hrs
4. Ice Window	V inf.	Two Tarn	12 hrs
5. Diamond Couloir	VI.	Two Tarn	10 hrs

Route	Standard	Starting Hut	Time
6. Southern Slabs.	VI inf.	Two Tarn	10 hrs
7. Diamond Buttress Original Route	VI	Two Tarn	15 hrs
8. Equator	VI sup., AI	Two Tarn	15 hrs
9. Diamond Buttress Direct	VI, A3	Two Tarn	15 hrs
10. Mediterranean	VI inf., A2	Two Tarn	15 hrs
11. South-West Ridge	IV	Two Tarn	9 hrs
12. Tower Ridge	V sup., A1.	Two Tarn	13 hrs
13. West Face	V	Two Tarn	10 hrs
14. Untravelled World	VI	Two Tarn	15 hrs
15. Misty Morning Couloir	VI	Two Tarn	9 hrs
16. West Ridge	V	Two Tarn/Kami	10 hrs
17. Northey Glacier	V	Kami Hut	10 hrs
18. North Face Standard Route	IV sup	Kami Hut	10 hrs
19. French Route	V sup., A1	Kami Hut	10 hrs
20. N.E. Buttress of Batian	V sup., A2	Austrian/Kami	10 hrs
21. Northern Slabs	VI inf., A2	Austrian/Kami	14 hrs
22. North Gate	VI	Austrian/Kami	16 hrs
23. East Gate	V sup	Austrian/Kami	13 hrs
24. N.E. Pillar of Nelion	V sup., A1	Austrian/Kami	14 hrs
25. Eastern Groove of Nelion	VI, A1	Austrian/Kami	16 hrs
26. Scott/Braithwaite	VII	Austrian/Kami	15 hrs
27. N E Face of Nelion	VI, A	Austrian/Kami	15 hrs
28. E Face of Nelion	VI, A13	Austrian/Kami	11 hrs
29. ESE Face of Nelion	VI, A2	Austrian/Kami	13 hrs
30. Mackinnon's Couloir	V sup	Austrian/Kami	8 hrs
31. Grand Traverse	VI	Two Tarn	3 days

ROUTES ON OTHER PEAKS

Route	Standard	Time
Thomson' Flake. Austrian Hut as base		
1. Only Route	VI	1/2 day
Point Melhuish, (4,880 m). Austrian Hut as base		
1. South-East Face	IV sup	1/2 day.
2. Via Diretta	III	1/2 day.
Point John, (4,883 m). Austrian Hut as base		
1. South-East Gully	III	1/2 day
2. South Ridge	IV inf.	1/2 day
3. South-West Face	A3	3 days
4. West Face	V sup., A4	3 days
5. North-West Arete	VI, A2	3 days
6. North Face	V sup., A4	3 days
7. Quo Vadis	VI	12 hrs
8. Point John Couloir	V	1/2 day
Point John Minor. Austrian Hut base		
1. Original Route	IV	1/2 day
2. South-East Ridge	V	1/2 day
Delamere Peak. Austrian Hut and Minto's Hut as bases		
1. South-East Face	III	1/2 day
2. North Face	II	1/2 day
Arthur's Seat, (4,666 m). Two Tarn Hut as base		
1. Styx	VI	8 hrs
Point pigott, (4,957 m). Two Tarn Hut as base		
1. N.W. Face	III	1/2 day
2. South Ridge	III sup	1/2 day
3. South Face	V	1/2 day
4. E.N.E. Ridge	V	1/2 day
5. West Face	IV	1/2 day
6. Tyndall Buttress	V	1/2 day
Midget Peak, (4,700 m). Two Tarn Hut Base		
1. South Gully	IV	1/2 day

2. S.S.W. Buttress.	IV sup	1/2 day
3. S.W. Gully	III sup	1/2 day
4. West Face	V., A2	1/2 day
5. Nek-Pad	IV	1/2 day
6. Nek-Line	V., A1	1/2 day
7. North Face	VI	1/2 day
8. S.E. Buttress	V inf.	1/2 day
9. Midget Minor	IV sup	1/2 day
10. Midget Minimus	V	1/2 day
11. Nek-Lace	V	1/2 day

Point Slade, (4,750 m). Two Tarn Hut as base

1. South Face.	V sup	1/2 day
2. The Great Slab	V	1/2 day
3. Speaker's Corner	V	1/2 day
4. East Rib	V	1/2 day

Point Dutton, (4885 m). Kami Hut as base

1. N.E. Face & Ridge	IV	1/2 day

Point Peter, (4,757 m). Kami Hut as base

1. N.E. Gully & Ridge	III	1/2 day
2. Window Ridge	VI A1	3/4 day
3. East Face Corner &	IV sup	1/2 day
N.E. Ridge		
4. South Ridge	IV	1/2 day
5. West Ridge	V sup., A1	1/2 day

Tereri, (4,714 m). Liki North Hut as base

1. South Face	III	1/2 day
2. W.N.W. Ridge	V	1/2 day

Sendeyo, (4,704). Liki North Hut as base

1. S.E. Chimney	III	1/2 day
2. N.E. Ridge	IV	1/2 day

Castle Rock, Teleki Valley Lodge as base

1. Only Route	IV	1/2 day

The Temple. Minto's Hut as base

1. Ricochette	VI	3/4 day

CLIMBING ROUTES

on

BATIAN (5,199 M)

and

NELION (5,188 M)

(1) **NORMAL ROUTE**

(via Nelion South Ridge, S.E. Face and Summit).

First ascent: E.E. Shipton and P. Wyn Harris, 6th Jan., 1929.
(ref. Alpine Journal Vol. 42 and Ice Cap No. 1)

Season: Christmas to mid-March.

Standard: IV inf. The route is rather complex, and much of the climbing is not above grade III. With difficult ice conditions the Gate of the Mists may be IV. An ice-axe and crampons are recommended. Throughout the climb care is needed to avoid dislodging loose stones.

Time: Allow 6-7 hours for the ascent of Nelion and a further 3 hours for reaching Batian and returning to Nelion. It's advisable to spend a night in the Howell Hut on Nelion's summit.

From the Austrian Hut cross the Lewis Glacier and scramble up the scree, which has many precariously balanced boulders and can be dangerous in half-light. Start climbing up a side groove about 55 m left of the obvious *Brocherel Couloir.* 18 m of easy climbing brings one to a wide, boulder-strewn terrace, at the left end of which is a gully *(Donkey Walk)* leading up to the left. Scramble up the gully for 25 m, then a mounting traverse back to the right up a series of easy ledges on the face. A move round a corner (III) leads to the foot of *Mackinder's Chimney.* Instead of climbing the chimney, descend 2½m and traverse right 6 m to a platform below the *Rabbit Hole* then climb a rib immediately right of the Rabbit Hole (III) and follow easy rocks to a platform at the top of Mackinder's Chimney. *One o'clock Gully* (quite easy, unless ice-filled) now leads up right for 40 m. Where it steepens, mount the left wall then traverse back right to reach block steps leading up to the crest of the main ridge. When it appears obvious, make a long traverse right across slab then up toward the base of *Mackinder's Gendarme.* A tin shelter (Baillie's Bivi), is found just below the notch beneath *Mackinder's Gendarme* on the main ridge. This is approximately half-way up Nelion. Turn the Gendarme on the left by first descending 7 to 10 m and then up a large gully. Most parties nowadays follow the De Graaf's Variation, which is the easiest and most direct route (IV inf.). Avoid Shipton's and Rickety Cracks by a traverse left for some 12 m out of a large gully, following the ascent of the square-cut groove for about 20 m, and then straightforward climbing to the ridge leading to the *Amphitheatre*.

Alternatively, instead of traversing 12 m out of the large gully, continue up the gully to two short chimneys known as *Shipton's Crack's* (IV inf.), which lead to a small platform *(Windy Gap)*, between the Gendarme and the main face. In recent years many parties have found the traverse of the Gendarme the easiest and quickest way of reaching Windy Gap. From Windy Gap climb 2 m over a bulge on the face to reach a ledge; follow this right until peters out on the main face. From here *Rickety Crack* (IV inf.) leads upwards for about 8 m to a platform. (A jammed nose of rock 2 m above the bottom of the crack can be used for protection on the first awkward exposed moves up the crack). Climb 30 m up a ridge to the right leading to a point overlooking the *Amphitheatre*.

Belay at the edge of the Amphitheatre and climb down 8 m to the right (III). Work round the back wall of the Amphitheatre to cracks leading up left into the bed of the gully. Ascend the gully, much loose rock, for two pitches to a platform. A 5 m wall is climbed by a shallow chimney (III), followed by a scramble over loose rock to a col overlooking the *Diamond Glacier*. Turn sharp right and up easy rocks to the summit of Nelion.

Variations: The Crack directly above Windy Gap has also been climbed out of season (Pfeffer and Pauer, August 1957). The chimney to the left of the point where the route traverses right into the Amphitheatre was climbed first by E. Sladen in 1938.

The summit of Batian is only 140 m away in a horizontal distance, but drop of nearly as many metres into the *Gate of the Mists* is involved. The ridge may be followed from Nelion, traversing down on the north side, then turning towards

Mount. Kenya. In the Gate of Mists.   *Iain Allan*

the Gate. Keep under an overhanging cliff and descend to a boss of rock just above the Gate. Climb down this (III or IV), possibly leaving a rope to facilitate the return, as there's usually ice in the cracks. Cross the snow in the Gate (which may be corniced); as the icework is less than a rope's length it is possible to belay from either side. Traverse round the base of the *Tower*, on its north side, up scree or snow, and over the ridge behind the Tower onto the South Face of Batian. Ledges lead left across the face into a gully. This is then followed to the summit, but if it's ice-filled take the wall to the right of the gully and chimney, taking care because of loose rock.

On the descent from Nelion there are many convenient places for roping down, as the number of abandoned slings and ropes indicate. Abseils undoubtedly save time, and parties generally descend De Graaf's Variation. The following description is probably the best way of descending from Nelion's summit. After having scrambled down easy rocks from the col overlooking the Diamond Glacier, instead of descending the 5 m shallow chimney, move right (facing outwards) to a platform a few metres down slabs. A block on this platform supports slings for a short abseil down the face towards Point Lenana. Some 15 m down, a small ledge has slings round a point of rock. Use these to make another 15 m abseil in the direction of Point John. This leads to easy rocks above the slabs leading down to the top of De Graaf's variation. One long abseil lead down this pitch to easy traversing over to Mackinder's Gendarme. One abseil leads down Mackinder's Chimney missing out the Rabbit Hole.

There is now a bolted abseiling route down Nelion. It starts in the same spot described above and follows a slightly different route. Follow arrows. Best done with 25 metre abseils.

Major variations: Two variations have been done to join the Normal Route at Mackinder's Gendarme.

Mount. Kenya. The Traverse to the base of Mackinder's Chimney on the Normal Route.   *Ian Howell*

(1a) **East Ridge**: This ridge of Nelion which rise from Flake Col consists of very loose shattered rock. Start 50 m left to the col and ascend ramp to ridge. The first four pitches are on poor rock and the fifth and sixth pitched are the most difficult. Climb the ridge then abseil into the top of the *Brocherel Couloir* and traverse to *Mackinder's Gendarme*. (A.G. Chinery and T. Weiker, 14th Jan. 1965. Grade IV sup.).

(1b.) **Brocherel Couloir**: This prominent couloir right of the Normal Route start was climbed by P. Snyder and R. Collister in 1974. Grade V.

(2) Mackinder's Route

First ascent: H.J. Mackinder with guide C. Ollier and porter J. Brocherel, 13th Sept., 1899. (ref. Geog. Journal Vol. XV, 1900, p.453)

Season: Christmas to mid-March.

Standard: IV. With the exception of Mackinder's Chimney, the rock does not exceed III. But, owing to the steepness and exposure of the Diamond Glacier (where crampons and possibly ice-pitons are needed), this route must be graded IV.

Time: Allow 8 hours for the ascent.

From the Austrian Hut follow the *Normal Route* as far as *Mackinder's Gendarme* (purist won't wish to by-pass *Mackinder's Chimney* which is IV). From the Gendarme descends scree to the left, and contour the base of the South Face of Nelion until the rocky rib overlooking the *Diamond Glacier* is reached. From this point join the South Face Route (No. 3), and follow it to the summit of Batian.

Recrossing the Diamond Glacier on the return in the afternoon can be very unpleasant and the Normal Route may be preferred for the descent.

(3) South Face Route

(via Darwin and Diamond Glacier).

During the last decade, in the June to October season, the South Face Route has become one of the most dangerous climbs on Mount Kenya. The reason why is simple. The Upper Darwin Glacier has virtually disappeared, leaving behind it blank, glazed rock slabs, which angle enough to hold covering snow. When viewed from the Teleki Valley or even from the base of the climb during these months, the appearance is seriously deceptive. The South Face Route looks to be in perfect condition.

It is strongly recommended to avoid the South Face Route. It does not exist in the form of the original route.
First ascent: A.H. Firmin and J.S. Bagenal, Feb. 1950. (ref. M.C.K. Bulletins 16, 1950; 44,1958; and 73,1975)
Season: Christmas to mid-March and June to October.
Standard: IV. In good conditions (i.e. when there's a good snow cover) the route doesn't exceed II. Owing to the Diamond Glacier however, a grade of IV is necessary.
Time: Allow 8 hours to Batian.

Either bivouac at the foot of the *Darwin Glacier* or make an early start from Two Tarn Hut.

The right tongue of the *Lower Darwin* is followed until movement left onto rocks appears more attractive. A narrow gully skirts the ice fall on the left. Continue up the left side of the *Upper Darwin* until the rocky rib overlooking the *Diamond Glacier* is reached. The Diamond Glacier can be crossed in several ways. Either cross it diagonally to the rocks of Batian (Mackinder's Party 1899), or head up towards the *Gate of the Mists* and join the *Normal Route* (De Graaf's Party 1952).

Variations: There are several important variations to this route.

1. At the point where the ill-defined ridge above the *Upper Darwin* peters out in the seamed South Face of Nelion, a shallow gully is climbed, and then out of this the route leads upwards on sound rock to reach the subsidiary summit of Nelion. From here descends to the small col and join the *Normal Route* (Grade V., R.W. Baillie and C. Rhys-Jones, January 1961).

Mount. Kenya. South Face. Showing Starts of Routes

David Keith Jones

2. Another variation follows the crack system to the right of
this (grade VI. A.Stott, F.Eastwood and R. Reid, January 1975).

3. The icefall between the *Lower and Upper Darwins* has been
climbed by a route up the right side (Grade V sup. P. Snyder,
I.F.Howell and J.Kiprono, Oct. 1974).

4. This icefall has also been ascended by a line just left centre
(Grade V sup. I. J. Allan and I.F.Howell, July 1975).

(4) **Ice Window Route**
Anyone attempting either the Diamond Couloir or the Ice
Window between Christmas and March is stretching the limits
of calculated risk.
First ascent: P. Snyder, Y. Laulan and B. LeDain, 20th Aug.,
1973. (ref. M.C.K. Bulletin 72, 1974).
Season: Christmas to mid-March and June to October.
Standard: V inf.
Time: 7 to 12 hours.
          This route is a true classic of the mountain. Either
bivouac beneath the *Darwin Glacier* or make an early start
from TwoTarn Hut.
          The Lower *Darwin Glacier* ascends into two bays.
The left-hand one (looking at the mountain) leads to the
Diamond Couloir, while the right-hand leads to the icefall which
joins the *Lower to the Upper Darwin Glacier*. The right-hand
bay is reached by a long traverse from the left at about mid-
height of the *Lower Darwin*. Ascend high into this bay and
belay at its top left-hand corner where a piece of old rope
hangs down. From this belay descend a few metre to gain a
slab leading left to gain a slab leading left. Go up this and a
corner which lead to a ramp going straight up. Follow this peg
belay on the right. Descend 5 m to the left to gain the narrow
Hidden Couloir. Ascend this to belay on left (at this point the
South Face Route branches off to the right). Two long pitches
straight up lead to a rock belay on the left shortly before a 6 m

icewall. Ascend this (V inf.) and continue up the couloir for another four pitches to gain the huge imposing ice cave. Move left inside the cave and cut an exit "window", if not already in place, and escape onto the lip of the *Diamond Glacier*. Up this directly in four long pitches to the *Gate of the Mists*.

A good selection of nuts and four ice-screws are sufficient for this route.

(5) **Diamond Couloir**
Anyone attempting the Diamond Couloir between Christmas and March is stretching the limits of calculated risk.
First ascent: P. Snyder and T. Mathenge, 4th and 5th Oct., 1973.(ref M.C.K. Bulletins 70,1972; 72,1974).
Season: Christmas to mid--March and June to October.
Standard: VI
Time: Allow 8 to 10 hours to the Gate of the Mists.

Probably the finest line on the mountain, this is the steep couloir which hangs from the lip of the *Diamond Glacier*.

The first icefall is steep and long , varying between 50 m and 70 m. Easier climbing follows for three rope length to the foot of another ice wall above which is the slope at the base of the *Headwall*. Surmount the ice wall by a pitch leading diagonally right to a rock belay, and then another pitch straight up towards the main Headwall. Traverse left across the slope to a small rock pillar in the centre of the couloir. A ramp leads up to the left and up a V-groove on the left of steep rocks, emerging on an ice slope directly below an ice cave (bivouac site). Traverse right from this cave onto the main *Diamond Glacier* and straight up to the *Gate of the Mists*.

Variations: The *Headwall* was climbed direct onto the Diamond Glacier, taking a line generally up the right side, then rising leftwards to the Glacier (Y. Chouinard and M.Covington, Jan. 1975).

A good selection of nut and four rock pegs, as well as four ice-screws should be carried on the Original Route. Nuts, rock pegs and ten ice-screws should be taken on the Headwall.

Mount Kenya. The South Face seen from the summit of Point John.
Showing Starts of Climbing Routes.   Ian Howell

(6) **Southern Slabs Route**

First ascent: R.W. Baillie and R.M.Kamke, 4th Jan., 1961. (ref. M.C.K. Bulletin 53, 1961).

Season: Christmas to mid-March.

Standard: VI inf.

Time: 10 hours

Start from Two Tarn Hut. This route follows a series of slabs which rise to the left of the *Diamond Couloir*. At points these slabs are interrupted by short steep sections, where the main difficulties lie.

Ascend the *Darwin Glacier* and climb the easy ramp immediately left of the foot of the *Diamond Couloir*. When some 12 m from Couloir climb a diedre (V), then up broken rock for 50 m onto a steep slab. Move left up this to break through the 'step' above, up to a large block. Traverse right around a rib onto another slab, and up this (V) to a stance under another 'step'. Traverse left onto corner and up to the foot of a bulging face split by a shallow groove which is climbed through a small overhang (VI inf.) and stance. Now traverse 30 m right into a gully and up this for another 30 m to a big ledge. Go right and climb shallow gully and slabs for 60 m. Then break through the overhang above by going left over a chockstone (V). Above and to the right is a large yellow face and some two rope lengths to the right of the left-hand edge is a concealed recess. Climb the recess (V) and traverse right and up the crack which may be iced. Descend to a broad ledge on the right and go along this to slab at the foot of a 5 m wall, which is climbed onto a large sloping ledge. Traverse right and down slightly to the base of a steep gully. Up to a sloping platform and hand swing left onto a loose looking block, and make a strenuous pull up onto the face above (V). Scramble right to the right-hand one to two steep gullies. Up this gully to join the *South-West Ridge* Route a little below the summit. Follow ridge to top.

A good selection of nuts and four rock pegs should be carried on this route.

(7) **Diamond Buttress Original Route**

First Ascent: D.J. Temple and I.F. Howell, 13th and 14th March, 1976.

Season: Christmas to mid-March.

Standard: VI. VII if tension traverse is climbed free. On the first ascent about 10 points of aid were used; subsequent ascents have eliminated all the aid, although most parties do the tension traverse on pitch 5.

Time: 15 hours.

This sustained route is one of the finest on the mountain. Start from Two Tarn hut.

The *Diamond Buttress* is the almost vertical 400 m wall between the *Southern Slabs Route* and the *South-west Ridge*. On the right side of the Buttress is a very prominent corner. Climb the corner up from the left where a long traverse then a short pendule gains the corner (IV). Two short pitches (VI and VI) lead to a wall. Move left and up to a V-chimney, climb this taking the left hand branch. Move right at top and up wall to ledge. Move right to crack and up this (VI), until the blank wall on the right can be crossed by tension traverse or free (VII). This leads into a chimney which is climbed to ledges (bivouac sites), then leftwards up slabs to obvious corner. Take traverse line leftwards for about 30 m to foot of crack; up this (VI). Now continue leftwards for several pitches (IV) to short chimney leading to leftwards sloping ramp/slab. Up this (V sup.) to prominent blank slab, then traverse right across steep wall, round corner into groove (V) and up to ledge (V). Traverse right to narrow crack, which is climbed (VI) to ledge. Up wall above and turn overhang by making strenuous move left (VI). Three easier pitches lead up to *South-West Ridge* which is followed to summit.

A good selection of nuts is adequate for this route.

Mount Kenya. The South Face. Showing Starts of Routes on the Diamond Buttress.

John Temple

(8) **Equator**

First ascent: I. J. Allan and I.F. Howell, 23rd, 24th and 25th Dec., 1979.(ref. M.C.K. Bulletin 76, 1980).

Season: Christmas to mid-March.

Standard: VI sup., A1.

Time: 15 hours to summit.

Right of centre and some 60 m up the *Diamond Buttress*, there's a light coloured feature formed by a steep slabs and a corner on the right. This is called *The Shield*. The corner on the right marks the line of the route.

Ascend the steep icy bay left of *Diamond Couloir* avalanche cone and gain a good, but small ledge, about 5 m above the icy slope and 30 m left of the *Diamond Buttress Original Route* start. From this ledge climb a corner on the left and climb more or less straight up for three pitches (VI, V, VI sup). These are all free . The third belay is hanging one and from here move right using three aid points (two bolts in place), to a ledge with a big block. One pitch straight up (poor rock and some aid points used), leads to a small bivouac site. Ascend slightly overhanging corner (five aid points), then up and left over bulge to sloping belay. Move right cross slab then up crack line to junction with *Diamond Buttress Original Route*. Move left, down, then up thin wall to blocks and ramp leading left. Belay at left end of ramp. Move right slightly and climb steep jam crack to fixed nut (VI). From this tension right to wider crack which leads up t belay. Opposite is obvious jam crack leading to ledge on right (VI). Move right behind flake and continue to base of shallow gully of doubtful rock. Up this (V) to reach large slab leading left to join *South-West Ridge*.

The final section of this climb, from the point where the route meets the junction with Diamond Buttress Original Route, was first climbed by R. K. Roschnik and A. J. Weatherhead, 17th Jan. 1968.

A good selection of nuts and a selection of six rock pegs should be carried.

(9) **Diamond Buttress Direct**

First ascent: I. F. Howell and I.J. Allan, 1st and 2nd Jan., 1978. (ref. M.C.K. Bulletin 75, 1978).

Season: Christmas to mid-March.

Standard: VI, A3.

Time: 15 hours

This route starts from the top left side of the *Darwin Glacier* where there are two pronounced snow ramps. From the upper ramp a prominent crack/faults system leads up rightwards to an obvious wide chimney feature. After this the route bears back leftwards, then straight up to join the *Diamond Buttress Original* route at the start of its third to last pitch. The *South-West Ridge* is then followed to the summit. The start of the route is approximately 120 m left of the *Diamond Buttress Original Route.*

Gain snow ramp by means of steep slabs and a 6 m corner (VI), which lead in from the left Cross ramp to wall which is climbed for 25 m (VI) to belay. Ascend crack on right (A1) and up to ledge. Move up flake system which leads up rightwards to top of big flake. Awkward moves right across wall (A1) to big block beneath chimney. Ascend chimney (A3) until it widens and follow to top (VI). Move up corner on right (IV sup.), then left to belay beneath steep crack. Up crack for 10 m (A1) then left 10 m ledges (bivouac site). Follow broken area leftwards for 20 m to obvious fault leading rightwards. Move up right, then continue to top of flakes. Follow steep wall above to belay in alcove (V). Move up 20 m to join the *Diamond Buttress Original* route at the leftward sloping slab/ramp. Follow this route to the summit.

A good selection of nuts plus six rock pegs (mainly blades) should be carried.

(10) **The Mediterranean route**

First ascent: M.A. Gallego and M.Gomez, 12th, 13th and 14th Feb., 1980.

Season: Christmas to mid-March

Standard: VI inf. A2.

Time: 3 days of first ascent.

This route is the furthest left of the *Diamond Buttress*

climbs. Start in the top left-hand corner of the ice-bay beneath the buttress. An ice couloir leads diagonally up left to a steep corner. Climb this and continue generally upwards for two more pitches, trending first left, then right, then left again to ledges and a recess (bivouac site). From here follow a corner, trending right, then continue up a wall starting with aid to join an overhanging corner, which again uses aid to reach a good ledge (bivouac sites). Move left more easily to the foot of the large prominent diedre. Do not ascend the diedre but take a smaller corner to the right which leads to the *"Butterfly"* feature. From the right side of the *"Butterfly"*, climb a small corner then easier rock leads to a belay. Move left to a corner which leads up to the foot of a big groove. From here move right to easy ground which is followed in two pitches to the junction of the South-West Ridge. Follow this to summit.

(11) **South-West Ridge Route**
First ascent: A. H. Firmin and J.W. Howard, 8th Jan., 1946 (ref. M.C.K. Bulletin 3, 1947; and 72,1974).
Season: Christmas to mid-March.
Standard: IV.
Time: 9 hours.

Start from Two Tarn Hut. Begin the climb near the top of the snow on the western side of the *Darwin Glacier*, where smooth, gentle slabs allow a rising traverse to be made into the notch between Point Slide and Batian. Easy climbing up the ridge until a traverse can be made across the amphitheatre to the ridge bounding the *West Face*. Up the ridge to a steep buttress and up this (IV) to the crest of the ridge. Follow this to Batian.

Variations: From the right side of the heed of the amphitheatre, traverse left for two pitches to a weakness in the wall above. One pitch (IV inf.) leads to the foot of a diedre. Up this, turning an overhang on the right (3 aid move), and then continue vertically (V sup.), then slightly left (3 aid moves) onto a block. Step right, and traverse (V), to the foot of a black corner. An elegant 35 m pitch (V) leads up this and the chimney above to the crest of the ridge (Merendi and Marimonti, Jan., 1958).

The *South-West Couloir* which descends from the amphitheatre was climbed by starting from the snout of the *Tyndall Glacier* and ascending the left wall to a stance beneath a steep corner. Then up the crack, move right onto slabs and up left to a scree-covered ledge. Left up the gully and wide crack above to large slab. Climb the short wall on the right and continue right on a slab above the main coulior to its "Y" junction. Move left up a tributary ramp leading to easy slabs and the amphitheatre (P. Snyder and C Barton, Feb. 1972, Grade V inf.).

The *South-West Coulior* has been climbed in winter conditions (grade V, P. Snyder and I.F. Howell, Oct. 1974).

(12) **Tower Ridge Route**
First ascent: Z. Drlik (solo), 5th and 6th Feb., 1980.
Season: Christmas to mid-March
Standard: V sup., A1.
Time: 13 hours.

This route ascends the prominent ridge, which splits the hanging glaciers of the *West Face*, from the snowfield / amphitheatre on the *South-West Ridge Route*. The climb begins from the Tyndall Glacier, left the obvious rock buttress located immediately left of the *South-West Couloir*. The route works its way up the left side of this buttress to gain the ridge proper approximately 100 m below the prominent *Lower Tower* (situated lower left side of snowfield/amphitheatre). The major difficulties are low down on the route. From the start, three pitches (IV sup., IV, V), lead to a belay beneath a leftward curving arch. The route then ascends the wall on the left of the arch (V sup.) then breaks rightwards (A1) through an overhang onto easier ground.

The route continues up, keeping left of the ridge, for three pitches (III, V, IV sup.), to reach the ridge proper beneath the *Lower tower*. One long pitch (IV inf.) reaches the very base of the Tower. The route then leads rightwards on easy ground (good bivouac site), around the base of the *Lower Tower* (II), then back leftwards above the Tower (II), to gain the ridge overlooking the *West Face*. Climb the ridge (II) to the *Upper Tower*, which is climbed direct (IV). Continue up the ridge for four pitches (III sup., IV, III), to reach the South West Ridge. Follow this to summit.

(13) **West Face Route**
First ascent: R.A. Caukwell and G.W. Rose, 7th Jan., 1955. (ref. M.C.K. Bulletins 33, 1955; 48, 1959; and 52, 1962).
Season: Mid-December to mid March and June to October.
Standard: V
Time: 10 hours.

Start from Two Tarn Hut. Ascend the *Tyndall Glacier* to the foot of a steep snow-slope rising up rightwards between the two hanging glaciers, *Forel* (left) and *Heim* (right). Then climb directly up the snow/icefield for about 250 m making for a rib on the upper part of the face which is not too evident. Most parties pass to the right of it. Climb up to the right to a cave (bivouac site), and either make a long traverse left to the gully (IV inf.) which leads up to the summit; or climb up the rock (V) trending right to the South-West Ridge.

The first three-quarters of the route require modern ice gear.

(14) **The Untravelled World**
First ascent: R. Barton and D. Morris, 10th and 11th Jan., 1978. (ref. M.C.K. Bulletin 75,1978).
Season: Mid-December to February.
Standard: VI.
Time: 15 hours.

This daring route is one of the most serious under-takings on the mountain.
Start from Two Tarn Hut. A very narrow ice gully leads from

the upper part of the *Tyndall Glacier* towards the left edge of the main serac barrier of the *Forel Glacier*. Climb this fully for four difficult pitches until an exposed traverse right allows one to gain a ramp, cutting rightwards through the seracs to the lower snowfields of the glacier. If this ramp is not present the serac barrier could perhaps be bypassed on the left. On the first ascent an excellent bivouac site was found in the bergschrund on the left. Climb the slopes above to the highest point of the *Forel*, which can actually appear as a tiny snow-field in its own right. An intricate mixed pitch leads to the upper slopes, and further mixed climbing trending slightly right, leads to the upper slope of the South-West Ridge some 20 m from the summit.

(15) **Misty Morning Couloir**

First ascent: A. Hyslop and J. Tinker, Sept. 1980.
Season: Probably best during June to October. The season is critical as the foot of the couloir is rarely linked to the Tyndall Glacier.
Standard: VI. The first ascent party felt the first two pitches warranted Scottish V.
Time: 9 hours climbing time. A bivouac was spent in bergschrund.

This couloir, which might be better described as an icicle, lies to the left of The Untravelled World Route, and joins the *Tyndall Glacier* with the extreme left side of the *Forel Glacier*. The first two pitches are very steep. The ice then becomes easier angled and in five more pitches provides an exit right onto the main Forel. The bergschrund bivouac cave of The Untravelled World is then reached, and this route is fol-lowed to the summit.

(16) **West Ridge Route**

First ascent: E.E. Shipton and H.W. Tilman, 1st Aug., 1930. (ref. Alpine journal 43 and Ice-Cap No. 1;cf. also Alpine Journal May 1949, and M.C.K. Bulletins 8, 1948; and 58; and 58, 1964).

Season: July to early October.
Standard: V.
Time: 10 hours.

Start from Kami Hut or bivouac at the snout of the *Cesar* and *Josef Glaciers*. Climb these glaciers to the *Firmin Col*. From here, steep ice and rock lead to the Petit Gendarme which is usually climbed by starting on the south side of the Gendarme, then traversing round north near the highest point. The ridge is descended on the north side to the gap behind the Gendarme. Now climb as far left a possible towards the *Upper Northey Glacier*, and tackle the *Grand Gendarme* by way of difficult slabs, until a corner on the right is turned and a wide ledge reached. This leads back to the ridge behind the *Grand Gendarme*. The ridge is followed to a 12 m pinnacle which is probably the crux of the route. Fine ridge climbing follows - not steep, but very broken to *Shipton's Notch*. Abseil into the Notch, climb out the other side, and follow ridge to summit.

Variations:
1. *Firmin Col* can be reached from Two Tarn Hut by ascending the *Tyndall Glacier* and climbing the couloir at its head. This is often difficult (Grade V).
2. An easy approach from Kami hut skirts the *Northey Glacier* and scramble up a gully between the *Petit Gendarme* and *Point Dutton*. Easy slabs lead from the col to the ridge.
3. Both the *Petit* and *Grand Gendarme's* have been climbed direct. In the case of the latter this is Grade VI.
4. *Shipton's Notch* can be bypassed by descending to an easy traverse line.

(17) **Northey Glacier Route**
First ascent: W.M. Adams and R.J.H. Chambers, 1st Feb., 1959. (ref. M.C.K. Bulletin 48,1959).
Season: Christmas to mid-March and June to October.
Standard: IV sup.
Time: 10 hours

From Kami Hut scramble to the base of the *Northey* then climb fairly easily to the *Ice-fall*. This 60 m section is the crux, and has been climbed by both its left and right sides. The *Upper Northey* is then ascended traversing off left to join the *North Face Standard Route* shortly above the Firmin Tower. Follow this route to summit.

Note: This route has probably changed substantially and care should be taken when climbing it.

(18) **North Face Standard Route**

First ascent: A.H. Firmin and P. Hicks, 31st July, 1944 (ref. Alpine Journal, 1945; and M.C.K. Bulletins 1, 1946; 45, 1958; and 53, 1961).
Season: July to October.
Standard: IV sup.
Time: 10 hours.

This route is the least difficult on the north side of the mountain. Start from Kami Hut, where a 40-minute walk below the foot of the North Ridge is made to the starting gully, which is marked by a cross in a circle chipped on rock. Climb straight up from the marker and move right at 6 m into the gully (IV inf.). Continue over easier rock until it's possible to scramble for 90 m up the gully to a steep wall. An obvious crack brings one onto a large terrace beneath a third steep wall (III sup) Climb 6 m up an easy gully on the left, traverse back into the centre, then straight up (III sup.) and scramble into the *Amphitheatre*. Scramble about 120 m across this until it steepens, in the direction of *Firmin's Tower*, which is at the top left-hand corner. Climb 25 m to a wide sloping ledge (III), then traverse right along the ledge for 20 m (III), until it is possible to gain the ridge on the left-hand skyline. A 9 m scramble brings one to the foot of *Firmin's Tower*. Climb the crack for 20 m to where it breaks into two branches. Chimney up the right-hand one for 15 m to the top of a massive loose block (overlooking

Mount Kenya. The North Face. Showing Starts of Routes.

David Keith Jones

the *Amphitheatre*). Move left into the original chimney and continue up for 9 m. Scramble for about 18 m and up to the top of the Tower (IV sup.). Descend to the ridge and scramble along it for 60 m until it steepens. Continue along the ridge for another 30 m (IV inf.). Move up to an obvious ledge then traverse right to a small Amphitheatre (III). Further scrambling brings one to the junction of the West ridge where there is a superb bivouac site. Whilst it is possible to climb along the ridge it is easier and safer to traverse horizontally from the bivouac site for about 120 m to *Shipton's Notch*. The rock in this area should be treated with care. This route is suitable for descent.

Variations:
1. On the crux section of *Firmin's tower* it's possible to move right from the loose block along an obvious ledge to the foot of a steep crack which is climbed direct (Grade V sup).
2. The *Firmin Tower* has been bypassed to the right with a difficult and exposed mixed pitch above the *Northey Glacier* (V), the main ridge being re-joined just above the Tower (A. Schoon and H. Graafland, July 1958).
3. A Japanese party made an ascent of the Kami Hut face of the North Ridge of Batian to join the *North face Standard Route* just below the tip of the gully before entering the *Amphitheatre* (1965).
4. The whole of the North Ridge was climbed by J. Moss and J. Linke in July 1974 (Grade V).
5. From the starting point of the *North Face Standard Route*, the grey rock area immediately left of the gully was climbed for 15 pitches to the base of *Firmin's Tower* (M. Anglada and party, August 1971).

(19) The French Route
First ascent: M. Martin and R.Rangaux, 28th Aug., 1952. (ref. La Montagne 359, Nov/Dec. 1952. cf. also M.C.K. Bulletins 26, 1953; 43,1957; 49, 1960; and 57, 1963).

Season: July to early October
Standard: V sup., A1.
Time: 10 hours.

Start from Kami Hut or bivouac beneath route. To the left of the start of the *North face Standard Route* there is a section of wall smoothed white by constant stone-fall; this wall leads to the platform of a gully. Start in the centre of this area. A 3 1/2 m corner leads to an easy traverse going right to a groove and chimney. Climb the chimney to the gully. Walk left up the gully for about 90 m to where the gully narrows and climb a groove by its right wall, which leads to easy ledges with a 1/2 m dyke. Follow the dyke to where it cuts the main gully, and at that point climb the right wall to a platform. Ascending traverse right to a corner, and follow this up for 45 m to emerge at the right-hand end of a scree-filled Amphitheatre. This Amphitheatre is bounded on its left by a wall formed by a ridge. This offers a natural line out of amphitheatre and can be followed from low down until it brings one to the red back wall of the Amphitheatre. Here there is a large platform at the foot of the thin steep *French Piton Crack*. Follow this for 12 m on aid (pegs usually in place), to an awkward stance. A traverse left for 3 m is made to the foot of a rib which is climbed (V sup.); and followed by a 3 m peg crack which leads to the back of a short deep chimney. This is climbed to the Upper Amphitheatre, from where about 100 m of climbing (III) leads to the West Ridge in the region of *Shipton's Notch*. Follow the West Ridge to the summit.

Variations:
1. After scrambling up the Lower Amphitheatre, the left-hand wall is climbed to the ridge. First, a crack is climbed which runs diagonally from left to right to the foot of a steep corner; then this 6 m corner is climbed to a very large square stance on a ledge. From here traverse across the 15 m wall on the left (G. B. Cliff and D. Rutowitz, July 1963).
2. At the top right-hand end of the Lower Amphitheatre, above some smooth slabs, there is a prominent chimney. This chim-

ney is climbed for about 180 m to emerge on the col behind the *Firmin Tower* on the *North Face Standard Route* (Grade VI, W.M. Adams and RA. Bennett, Aug., 1959).

3. From the foot of the above mentioned Chimney, the steep wall on the right is climbed to reach the foot of the *Firmin Tower* (Grade VI, I.J. Allan and M. Savage, June 1972).

(20) **North-East Buttress of Batian**

First ascent: I.F. Howell, P.Snyder and I.J. Allan, Feb. 1976.
Season: January to mid-March and June to October.
Standard: V sup., A1.
Time: 10 hours.

Start from either Kami Hut or Austrian Hut. On the north-east side of the mountain there is a huge gully falling beneath the *Gate of the Mists* and splitting Batian and Nelion. This gully is distinguished by two prominent *Lower and Upper Amphitheatres*. From the right side climb two pitches (III), into the Lower Amphitheatre. From this point the route breaks out rightwards making for a prominent corner. Four pitches (IV) lead to this corner. Ascend corner for 100 m (V), to reach a notch in the ridge. Follow this ridge to the foot of the *French Piton Crack*, and continue up the *French Route* to the summit.

A good selection of nuts and approximately four rock pegs should be carried on this route.

(21) **Northern Slabs Route**

First ascent: I.F. Howell and D.J Temple, 11th and 12th Feb., 1973. (ref. M.C.K. Bulletin 71, 1973).
Season: January to March and June to October.
Standard: VI inf., A2.
Time: 14 hours.

Start from either Kami Hut or Austrian Hut. Follow the *North-East Buttress of Batian Route* as far as the *Lower Amphitheatre*. Scramble up to the steep back-wall. Start this wall about centre and trend up rightwards to the base of an obvious chimney (IV sup.). Ascend a crack just left of the

chimney (V), then step left to the slab. Surmount bulge above
(one aid move), then difficult move left (VI inf,), and continue
leftwards for 8 m until it is possible to climb straight up.
Continue direct for about 80 m to big ledge. Move left into
Upper Amphitheatre, and leftward up obvious gully 80 m until a
natural break leads out right across slabs. Cross these easy-
angled slabs for several rope lengths, then move up to overhanging corner. Climb this (A1) and the easy chimney above
to another belt of slabs leading leftwards. Cross these
(bivouac sites), to a monolith, and climb the crack between the
monolith and the wall (A2). Follow stepped ledges leftwards
for two pitches, then make an awkward move round a rib (V) to
the base of a smooth wall. Climb the crack through the overhang (A1) for 10 m to a belt of overhangs. Ascend overhang
(one aid move), then up left and round rib (VI inf.), to base of
chimney. Up this (V inf.), to easy ground which is climbed for
120 m to join the West Ridge just left of *Shipton's Notch*.
Follow the West Ridge to the summit.

      The second ascent party did the route entirely with nuts.

(22) **North Gate**
First ascent: I.J. Allan and I.F. Howell, 31st Aug. and 1st Sept.
1980.
Season: June to October.
Standard: VI.
Time: 16 hours.

      This very fine route takes the *"super-couloir"* on the
north of the mountain which splits Nelion and Batian. Parties
attempting it should be fit and acclimatised, and able to move
quickly up the middle section of the route where stonefall danger from the *Gate of the Mists* is considerable.

      Start as for the *North-East Buttress of Batian*, and
gain the *Lower Amphitheatre* (III, III). At the left back corner of
this Amphitheatre is a prominent slanting crack-line.

      Climb this in four pitches (VI, VI, IV, II), to gain the
upper Amphitheatre, below the *Gate of the Mists*. Scramble up

Mount Kenya. Climbing on the North-East Buttress of Batian.

Iain Allan

this for 70 m, then two dangerous pitches lead to a belay in the middle of the back wall (IV, IV). Traverse right along a ledge to gain the right-hand corner, up this, then mantle shelves lead to a niche below large clean slabs, (IV sup., V). Traverse right and down slab (VI), then up crack system to belay on big ledge on right. Continue up for two pitches (IV sup., VI), the second of which commences with an awkward move left to slabs above. Up these trending right to easier ground. A chimney (V, V), leads to a crack leading left (V), to a bivouac site beneath a wide chimney. Up this, through the *"keyhole"* (V), then move right and up steeping ground (VI) to finish on the West Ridge 15 m below the summit of Batian.

A good selection of nuts are needed for this route.

(23) **East Gate**

First ascent: I.F. Howell and P.Brettle, 20th and 21st July, 1980.
Season: June to October.
Standard: V sup. Only two moves are this standard.
Time: 13 hours.

This route takes the steep wall on Nelion just to the left of the *Gate of the Mists* on the north side. Start 10 m right of the *North-East Pillar of Nelion start*. Three pitches lead up into the Amphitheatre, then one up left to the arete. Continue up the arete for two pitches, first an awkward chimney, then a groove on the left. Scrambling leads to the right-hand of two obvious grooves (the left one is on the *North-East Pillar of Nelion*). Up this for one pitch then move down and right across a slab under an overhang (V) and squeeze past a flake to a groove leading up and slightly right. Up this for a pitch and a half to a good bivouac site. From left side of ledge continue in groove line trending slightly right. Traverse easily left to short steep corner on *North-East Pillar Route*. Up this (V), the immediately right and continue up and right for two and a half pitches to a large bivouac ledge below the upper *"pillar"*. Move right across a dirty wet gully and up to a good but small bivouac

Mount Kenya. The North-East Face of Nelion. Showing the starts
of Routes from the Krapf Glacier   Iain Allan.

ledge (water available). Above is a smooth wall broken on the left by a clean crack and on the right by a broken crack "stair-case pitch". Up this (V sup.), to sloping ledge. Move right to arete, and up this, surmounting blocks, to easier ground. Two excellent pitches. Move left then up to summit.

A good selection of nuts should be taken. Pegs are not necessary.

(24) North-East Pillar of Nelion

First ascent: G.B.Cliff and D.Rutowitz, 2nd, 3rd and 4th Aug. 1963. (ref. м.с.к. Bulletins 57, 1963; and 63, 1966).
Season: June to early October.
Standard: V sup.A1. The route has been climbed completely free at Grade VI sup.
Time: 14 hours.

This very fine route starts at the foot of the nose of Nelion, which is a prominent series of pillars left of the huge gully and amphitheatres which divide Nelion from Batian.

The route threads its way up these pillars, starting at a crack on the extreme right end of the 90 m wall which faces east and buts onto the *Krapf Glacier*. The first obstacle on the climb is the *Hourglass Crack* which is immediately opposite a large block set into the *Krapf Glacier* some 15 m from the wall itself. Avoid the first part of the Crack by climbing the wall well to its left and by easy traversing enter the Crack at about 25 m. The Crack then widens and it's climbed until an exit is barred by overhanging blocks. A break left is made and the ridge is reached. This followed for 15 m to join the Ramp, which is climbed for 120 m to the foot of the *Grey Pillar*, the most promi-nent feature on the face. An ascending traverse right, round the corner of the Pillar, brings two cracks into view.

The first and less obvious crack *(Sinister Crack)*, some 90 m in length, is climbed in four pitches. Ignore the obvious crack and climb the large loose blocks on the left to a stance with a large block belay. The second pitch (20 m), involves an awkward off-balance move over a groove into the

Mount Kenya. The North-East Face of Nelion. Showing the starts of Routes.

Peter Brettel

Sinister Crack itself (only now obvious), and leads to an excellent stance. The crack on the right wall is now followed for 12 m to a small square stance next to a large loose flake. The crack now becomes harder and is climbed for 40 m to a good stance. Easy climbing for 30 m, followed by a traverse left, brings the shoulder of the Pillar. Continue up large broken slabs to a steep corner, which is climbed for 15 m on aid (A1). Above is a large overhanging orange-coloured wall (good bivouac sites beneath)

From this point traverse left to a large, very steep, holdless grey slab called the *Catwalk*. Climb the crack just right of centre of the slabs to a peg, then tension-traverse across the slab. Once across the slab a 6 m groove leads up to large square stance beneath the final chimney. This 6 m chimney enters a gully above which, after a short steep section easy of scrambling leads to the summit of Nelion.

A good selection of nuts, from small wires to big sizes should be carried on this route.

(25) **Eastern Groove of Nelion**
First ascent: I.F. Howell and I. J. Allan, 2nd and 3rd June, 1978.
Season: June to October.
Standard: VI, A1. or VII.
Time: 16 hours.

This sustained route which has been climbed free is one of the finest on the mountain.

On the *Krapf Glacier*, some 60 m to the left side of the recess which leads to the *Lower Amphitheatre* splitting Nelion from Batian, and 15 m left of the *North-East Pillar Route*, this route starts to be a very smooth slab. Ascend slab which leads to further slabs and cave. Exit left from cave onto slabs which are ascended bearing slightly right to an arm wing up and round to the right (V). Belay 6 m higher in a niche. Move up to vertical steep crack, climb this (one aid point), then continue up leftwards sloping ramp until awkward mantle shelf is made right (VI), and up to bottom of off-width crack. Up this (one aid point), to belay and easier ground to large shelf. Move left along this for nearly 90 m to a point some 15 m right of the left end of the shelf. The *Eastern Groove* itself can be seen above and slightly right of this point and is the shallow square-cut groove forming the next main feature left of the *Grey Corner on the Scott-Braithwaite Route*. Two pitches (IV sup., V sup.) lead to the bottom of the Groove. The first curved rightwards and has some doubtful rock. The second is shorter and follows a crack and wall to a belay at the foot of the Groove. The start is blank and needs some five aid points until it relents to jamming and bridging (VI). Another pitch (VI) leads to ledges (poor bivouac site). Two more pitches each with occasional aid points lead to a belay at the foot of a layback crack. Ascend this (Vsup) and move left to a phallic rock. Behind this, slabs lead to a vertical corner crack which is voided by an off-width crack round the corner on to the left. Climb this with some aid points, then move back right and up to easier ground, which leads in two pitches (IV and III) to a large terrace. Follow this right for one pitch to a scree gully and ascend this, then right up chimney to easier ground leading to summit.

The third ascent party which climbed the route entirely free, did not move left to the phallic rock. They climbed more or less straight up avoiding the aided off-width (E.Hart, M. Christensen and M. Hafner, July 1979).

(26) **Scott-Braithwaite Route**
First ascent: D. Scott and P. Braithwaite, 3rd and 4th Oct. 1976.
Season: June to October.
Standard: VII.
Time: 15 hours.

This very difficult route takes a direct line from the *Krapf Glacier* up Nelion to the *Grey Corner*. The cracks in this corner are then climbed. The route then joins the *North-East Pillar Route* taking in the 15 m corner and the *Catwalk*. The route then continues independently up left to the top of Nelion. The climb starts about 50 m left of the *Eastern Groove Route* at an obvious fracture up the 90 m wall. For three pitches ascend prominent steep grooves turning overhangs first on the left then the right (VII). Cross the scree ledges and climb up to the foot of the *Grey Corner* (IV sup). Climb the cracks on the right wall of this Corner for 50 m to a hanging block (VI). Turn the block on the right (VII), and enter the off-width crack which is climbed for 16 m. Continue over easier ground to a short corner, which is climbed (VI) to join the *North-East Pillar Route* beneath the 15 m corner. Follow this route past the Catwalk and the 6 m chimney above, then trend leftwards (V) to summit.

A good selection of nuts from small wires to large sizes should be carried.

(27) **North-East Face of Nelion**
First ascent: I.F. Howell and R.F. Higgins. 16th and 17th July, 1969.
Season: June to October and perhaps Christmas to mid-March.
Standard: VI.
Time: 15 hours.

This route starts at the same point as the *North-East Buttress of Batian route*, and follows the two grade III pitches into the *Lower Amphitheatre*; it then continues up the scree slopes of this Amphitheatre and traverse easily across left-wards to the side of Nelion. Obvious ledges lead across left-wards (III), to the scree covered ramp above the 90 m wall, on Nelion's North-East Face. Follow the ramp as far left as possible past the *Grey Corner* on the *Scott-Braithwaite route* and the *Eastern Groove*. Two short pitches (V sup, V.), are climbed up crack lines from very nearly the highest point on the ramp to gain a better ledge. One long pitch (V), leads to a ledge and blocks. Move right to some parallel cracks (VI), which are climbed to a small sloping ledge. Move left into a groove and climb this to a good ledge. Climb a short steep wall (V) to another ledge, then climb a broken jam crack (VI) to a ledge and blocks. Move up and right onto a spiralling slab and move left into a scoop, and so onto a large sloping ledge (VI). Poor bivouac site. Move right round flake and climb rotten cracks in *Grey Chute* (V), and move back left to a ledge. Up more broken rocks to large ledges leading into the funnel of the *East Face Route* (good bivouac ledge). Ascend one pitch on the left side of the funnel and then move right and up (V) to a large ledge beneath the final overhanging wall.   Follow this ledge right to join the finishing gully of the *North-East Pillar Route* which leads to the summit.

A good selection of nuts and few rock pegs should be carried.

(28) **East Face Route**

First ascent: H.Klier, S. Aeberli and G.B. Cliff, 7th Aug. 1963. (ref. м.с.к. Bulletin 57, 1963).
Season: Christmas to mid-March and June to October.
Standard: VI, A3.
Time: 11 hours.

In the centre of the East Face of Nelion a series of cracks run down from the summit to the *Krapf Glacier*. Halfway up the wall these cracks lead into a funnel, above which the final wall towers. From the Glacier the first two pitches of the crack are in a corner which leads to a good stance beneath the third pitch, which is a series of overhangs. This third pitch *(The Inverted Staircase)*, is the crux of the climb (VI) and leads to the continuation of the main crack topped by another overhang. The crack then opens to form a good stance, then the right wall is followed for 15 m, where a 3 m traverse left is made. Climb over loose block to the *Raven's Nest* - a fine bivouac site. One pitch in the crack on the right brings one to a large split block which is climbed to a stance. After three steps to the right an overhanging cleft is climbed (VI), with an awkward section above. The crack is followed for 6 m, then a traverse left round a corner gives a good stance. Continue up 5 m

Mount Kenya. Aerial View.   *J. I. Moore*

then break left to an overhang which is climbed free, and a slab then leads across into the tip of the funnel. The groove is climbed for three pitches, followed by one more pitch on the left side which leads to easier climbing. From here the *Black Crack* can be seen, leading up to the last overhang of the final wall. The base of the Crack is reached by climbing a series of cracks and ledges from left to right for two pitches. The Black Crack starts in a chimney (VI inf.) for 15 m and continues overhanging and smooth for 10 m (VI, A3), and leads to a good ledge on the left. One more pitch (3 aid moves) leads to easy angled rocks to the summit.

A good selection of nuts and 6 rock pegs should be carried.

(29) **East-South-East Face of Nelion.**

First ascent: I.F. Howell and D.J. Temple, 20th and 21st March 1976.
Season: Christmas to mid-March and June to October.
Standard: VI, A2.
Time: 13 hours.

This rather forced route begins at the foot of *Mackinnon's Couloir*, 30 m left of the *East Face Route*. Climb the steep wall then move left, surmounting a small roof on aid, to the bottom of a steep chimney. Ascend this (V sup.), to attain ledge system trending left into big couloir. Up this for two rope lengths with aid over a difficult section. Traverse right, out of gully onto easier ground on slabby rock and a bivouac site. Climb the flake recess and exit right (aid). Easy climbing up to big ledges at the foot of the *East Face Headwall*. Up chimney to a large block ledge below the *Black Crack of the East Face Route*. Move left to a very steep slab below an overhang, this is traversed left (A2) for one pitch, then directly upward for two pitches. Move right to crack and follow this to scree below summit.

(30) **Mackinnon's Couloir.**

First ascent: P. Snyder and P. MacGowan, 14th March , 1973.
Season: Christmas to mid-March
Standard: V sup.
Time: 8 hours.

Start from the Austrian Hut or Kami Hut. It should be noted that there's considerable stonefall danger if there are parties on the *Normal Route*. This couloir which lies between the East Face of Nelion and the East ridge on the north side is climbed for four pitches (ice and rock) to a fork. Take the right fork, and two pitches (ice), lead to an amphitheatre, and the couloir above is ascended to a cave. Move right and up to a block belay, then after a delicate step right (v sup),attain a subsidiary ridge overlooking two amphitheatres, which lead up to join the *Normal route*. Cross this on easy ledges, up chimney, then right and up a steep hard corner (Vsup.). Move right to gully, then back left up ramp leading to subsidiary summit of Nelion.

(31) **Grand Traverse of**
Point Pigott, Batian, Nelion and Point John.

First completion: R.W.Baillie and T.Phillips, March 1964.
Season: Christmas to mid-March June to October.
Standard: VI.
Time: 3 days.

The *South Ridge of Point Pigott* is climbed to the summit of this peak. The *East-North-East Ridge of Point Pigott* is then descended to the Firmin Col (bivouac site). The *West Ridge of Batian* is then ascended to the summit, and the *Normal Route* followed across to Nelion and down the South-East Face to *Mackinder's Gendarme*. The South Ridge crest of Nelion is descended to meet Point John, which is climbed to the summit. Descend the *South-East Gully of Point John*.

Topographical Diagrams
of
Selected Routes
on
Batian and Nelion

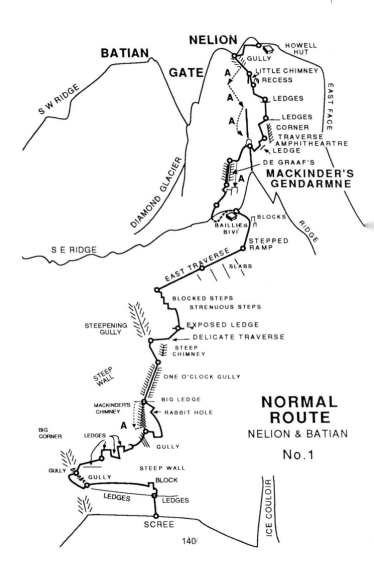

BATIAN

NELION

GATE

SW RIDGE

HOWELL HUT

GULLY

LITTLE CHIMNEY
RECESS

EAST FACE

LEDGES

LEDGES
CORNER
TRAVERSE
AMPHITHEARTRE
LEDGE

DE GRAAF'S

MACKINDER'S
GENDARMNE

DIAMOND GLACIER

BAILLIES
BIVI'

BLOCKS

RIDGE

SE RIDGE

STEPPED
RAMP

EAST TRAVERSE

SLABS

BLOCKED STEPS
STRENUOUS STEPS

STEEPENING
GULLY

EXPOSED LEDGE

DELICATE TRAVERSE

STEEP
CHIMNEY

STEEP
WALL

ONE O'CLOCK GULLY

MACKINDER'S
CHIMNEY

BIG LEDGE

RABBIT HOLE

A

NORMAL
ROUTE

NELION & BATIAN

No.1

BIG
CORNER

LEDGES

GULLY

GULLY

GULLY

STEEP WALL

BLOCK

LEDGES

LEDGES

SCREE

ICE COULOIR

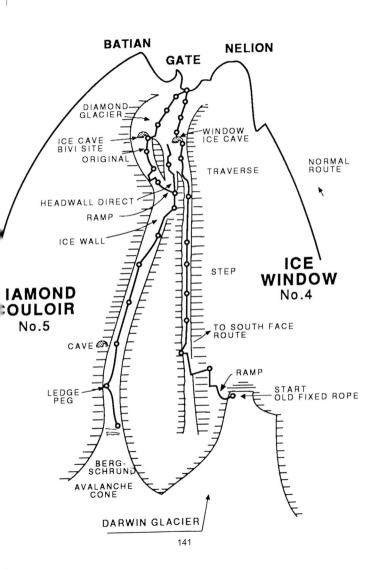

BATIAN

NELION

GATE

DIAMOND
GLACIER

WINDOW
ICE CAVE

ICE CAVE
BIVI SITE

NORMAL
ROUTE

ORIGINAL

TRAVERSE

HEADWALL DIRECT

RAMP

ICE WALL

STEP

ICE
WINDOW
No.4

DIAMOND
COULOIR
No.5

CAVE

TO SOUTH FACE
ROUTE

LEDGE
PEG

RAMP

START
OLD FIXED ROPE

BERG-
SCHRUND

AVALANCHE
CONE

DARWIN GLACIER

MOUNT KENYA AND KILIMANJARO

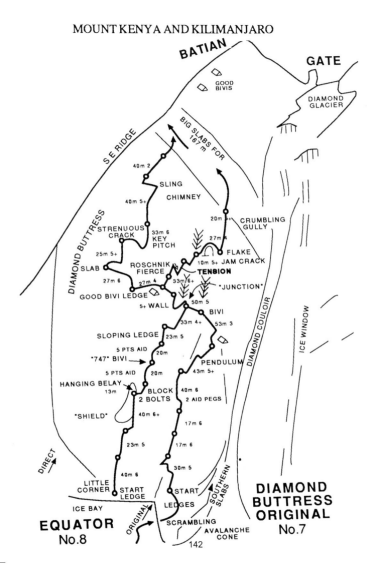

BATIAN

GATE

GOOD BIVIS

DIAMOND GLACIER

S E RIDGE

BIG SLABS FOR 167m

40m 2

SLING CHIMNEY

40m 5+

20m 5+ CRUMBLING GULLY

27m 4

DIAMOND BUTTRESS

STRENUOUS CRACK

33m 6 KEY PITCH

FLAKE

25m 5+

ROSCHNIK FIERCE

10m 5+ JAM CRACK

SLAB

27m 4

TENSION

27m 6

33m 6+

"JUNCTION"

GOOD BIVI LEDGE

5+ WALL

50m 5

BIVI

SLOPING LEDGE

33m 4+

53m 3

23m 5

5 PTS AID

20m

"747" BIVI

PENDULUM

5 PTS AID

20m

43m 5+

HANGING BELAY

13m

BLOCK 2 BOLTS

40m 6

2 AID PEGS

"SHIELD"

40m 6+

17m 6

DIRECT

23m 5

17m 6

LITTLE CORNER

40m 6

START LEDGE

30m 5

START LEDGES

ICE BAY

ORIGINAL

SCRAMBLING

SOUTHERN SLABS

DIAMOND COULOIR

ICE WINDOW

DIAMOND BUTTRESS ORIGINAL No.7

EQUATOR No.8

AVALANCHE CONE

142

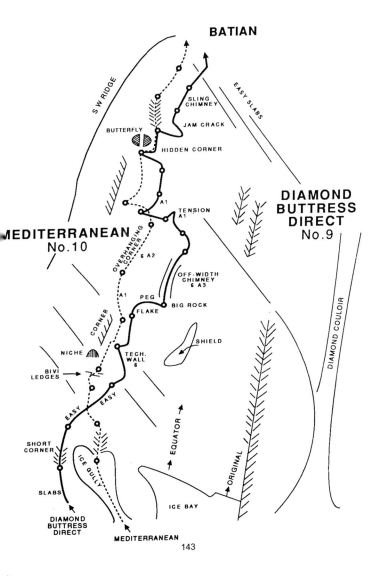

BATIAN

SW RIDGE

EASY SLABS

SLING CHIMNEY

JAM CRACK

BUTTERFLY

HIDDEN CORNER

A1

DIAMOND BUTTRESS DIRECT
No.9

TENSION A1

MEDITERRANEAN
No.10

OVERHANGING CORNER

6 A2

OFF-WIDTH CHIMNEY 6 A3

CORNER

A1

PEG

FLAKE

BIG ROCK

NICHE

SHIELD

BIVI LEDGES

TECH. WALL 6

EASY

EASY

DIAMOND COULOIR

EQUATOR

ORIGINAL

SHORT CORNER

ICE GULLY

SLABS

DIAMOND BUTTRESS DIRECT

ICE BAY

MEDITERRANEAN

143

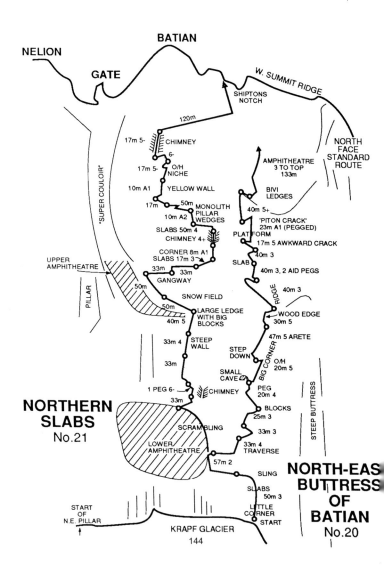

NELION

BATIAN

GATE

W. SUMMIT RIDGE

SHIPTONS NOTCH

NORTH FACE STANDARD ROUTE

"SUPER COULOIR"

120m

17m 5-   CHIMNEY

6-

17m 5-   O/H NICHE

10m A1   YELLOW WALL

17m   50m   MONOLITH PILLAR WEDGES

10m A2

SLABS 50m 4
CHIMNEY 4+

CORNER 8m A1
SLABS 17m 3

UPPER AMPHITHEATRE

33m   33m   GANGWAY

PILLAR

50m   SNOW FIELD

50m   LARGE LEDGE WITH BIG BLOCKS

40m 5

33m 4   STEEP WALL

33m

1 PEG 6-

33m   CHIMNEY

NORTHERN SLABS
No. 21

SCRAMBLING

LOWER AMPHITHEATRE

AMPHITHEATRE 3 TO TOP 133m

BIVI LEDGES

40m 5+

'PITON CRACK' 23m A1 (PEGGED)

PLATFORM

17m 5 AWKWARD CRACK

40m 3

SLAB

40m 3, 2 AID PEGS

40m 3

WOOD EDGE

RIDGE

30m 5

47m 5 ARETE

STEP DOWN

BIG CORNER   O/H 20m 5

SMALL CAVE

PEG 20m 3

BLOCKS

25m 3

33m 3

33m 4   TRAVERSE

57m 2

STEEP BUTTRESS

SLING

SLABS 50m 3

LITTLE CORNER

START

NORTH-EAST BUTTRESS OF BATIAN
No. 20

START OF N.E. PILLAR

KRAPF GLACIER

144

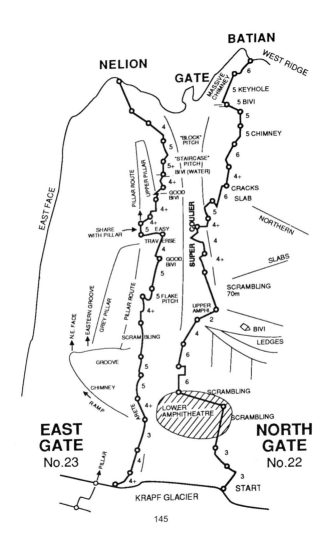

BATIAN

NELION

GATE

WEST RIDGE

MASSIVE CHIMNEY

6

5 KEYHOLE

5 BIVI

5

5 CHIMNEY

6

4+

CRACKS SLAB

6

5

4+

NORTHERN

"BLOCK" PITCH

"STAIRCASE" PITCH
BIVI (WATER)

GOOD BIVI

EAST FACE

PILLAR ROUTE

UPPER PILLAR

4

5

5+

4+

4+

5 EASY

SHARE WITH PILLAR

TRAVERSE

GOOD BIVI

5

5 FLAKE PITCH

4+

SUPER COULIER

4+

SLABS

SCRAMBLING 70m

UPPER AMPHI

2

N.E. FACE

EASTERN GROOVE

GREY PILLAR

PILLAR ROUTE

SCRAMBLING

4

6

BIVI

LEDGES

GROOVE

5

5

CHIMNEY

RAMP

ARETE

4+

3

6

6

SCRAMBLING

LOWER AMPHITHEATRE

SCRAMBLING

EAST GATE
No. 23

PILLAR

4+

4

3

3

3

NORTH GATE
No. 22

START

KRAPF GLACIER

145

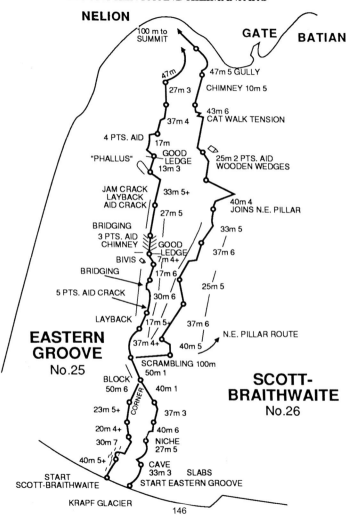

MOUNT KENYA AND KILIMANJARO

NELION

GATE

BATIAN

100 m to SUMMIT

47m

27m 3

37m 4

47m 5 GULLY

CHIMNEY 10m 5

43m 6 CAT WALK TENSION

4 PTS. AID

17m

GOOD LEDGE

25m 2 PTS. AID WOODEN WEDGES

"PHALLUS"

13m 3

JAM CRACK LAYBACK AID CRACK

33m 5+

40m 4 JOINS N.E. PILLAR

27m 5

33m 5

BRIDGING 3 PTS. AID CHIMNEY

GOOD LEDGE

37m 6

BIVIS

7m 4+

BRIDGING

17m 6

5 PTS. AID CRACK

30m 6

25m 5

LAYBACK

17m 5+

37m 6

EASTERN GROOVE No. 25

37m 4+

40m 5

N.E. PILLAR ROUTE

SCRAMBLING 100m

50m 1

BLOCK

50m 6

40m 1

SCOTT-BRAITHWAITE No. 26

23m 5+

CORNER

37m 3

20m 4+

30m 7

40m 6

NICHE

27m 5

40m 5+

CAVE

33m 3

SLABS

START SCOTT-BRAITHWAITE

START EASTERN GROOVE

KRAPF GLACIER

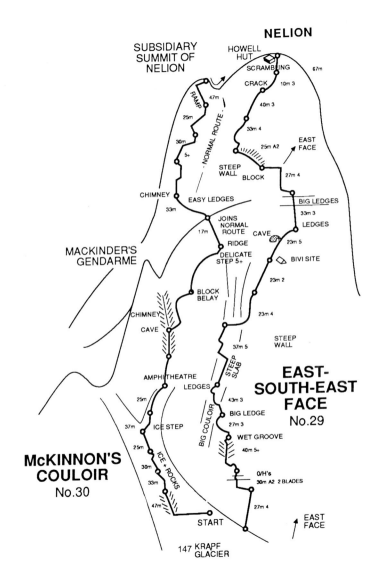

NELION

SUBSIDIARY SUMMIT OF NELION

HOWELL HUT

SCRAMBLING

CRACK

67m

10m 3

RAMP

40m 3

47m

33m 4

25m

25m A2

EAST FACE

30m

5+

STEEP WALL

BLOCK

27m 4

CHIMNEY

EASY LEDGES

33m

BIG LEDGES

JOINS NORMAL ROUTE

33m 3

17m

LEDGES

CAVE

MACKINDER'S GENDARME

RIDGE

23m 5

DELICATE STEP 5+

BIVI SITE

23m 2

BLOCK BELAY

23m 4

CHIMNEY

37m 5

STEEP WALL

CAVE

AMPHITHEATRE

LEDGES

STEEP SLAB

EAST-SOUTH-EAST FACE
No.29

25m

43m 3

37m

ICE STEP

BIG LEDGE

27m 3

BIG COULOIR

25m

WET GROOVE

McKINNON'S COULOIR
No.30

30m

ICE + ROCKS

40m 5+

33m

O/H's

30m A2 2 BLADES

47m

27m 4

START

EAST FACE

147 KRAPF GLACIER

CLIMBS FROM AUSTRIAN HUT

Point Lenana (4,985 m), the third highest peak of the mountain is accessible from Top Hut or the Austrian Hut via its SW Ridge in less than an hour. No technical climbing is involved but care should be exercised and parties should not stray left onto the Lewis Glacier, unless roped. In the upper part, where movement left off the rocks is necessary, steps cannot always be kicked and an ice-axe may be needed. Point Lenana may also be reached from the north, but this route involves some Grade I climbing for a pitch or two in the upper part to reach the NW Ridge of Lenana.

Point Thomson (4,955 m), can be reached from Lenana along the snow ridge at the head of the Lewis and Gregory glaciers but there are some crevasses here, and parties should be roped. The peak itself is an easy scramble.

Thomson's Flake: This spectacular pinnacle situated between Point Thomson and the East Ridge of Nelion has been climbed by a worthwhile route. Start from the col between the Flake and Point Thomson, and descend to foot of chimney. Climb corner on left to ramp, then traverse left along ramp to corner and climb it to second platform. Climb short wall direct to second ramp, and traverse right to a shoulder. Traverse along ridge and step round corner and continue traverse for 3 m. Ascend overhang to belay in crack, then break out right onto summit ridge, which is followed to summit. Abseil down south side. (First ascent: L. Herncarek, W. Welsch and B Cliff, Sept. 1962. Grade VI).

Point Melhuish (4,880 m), across the Lewis Glacier from Austrian Hut is an easy scramble from the NE. Two worthy route are situated on the SE side.

1. South-East Face

      The Lewis Glacier face of Melhuish is divided into two by an edge of overhangs and ceilings. The climb is mainly on the face to the left of this edge, breaking through some overhangs near the top. The climb is in six pitches, mostly of low standard. (First ascent: R. M. Kamke and W. M. Boyes, Dec. 1960. Grade IV sup.).

2. Via Diretta

      This climb goes straight up the easy angled slabs on the South-East Face, taking a line immediately beneath the summit. Start just right of a prominent rib. (First ascent: G. Moseley and T. Manhire, Jan. 1965. Grade III).

Point John (4,883 m). This beautiful peak offers some classic routes.

1. South-East Gully

First ascent: E E Shipton and R E G Russel, 18th Dec. 1929.
Standard: III
Time: Half a day.

      Climb the prominent wide gully on the SE Face. Take the right-hand branch leading to the main ridge at a prominent sharp V-notch. The most difficult parts are just before reaching the main ridge, and from here to the summit. **Variation**: Where the gully branches, the left-hand route may be taken. This gully, less clearly defined, joins the other route on the summit ridge. (Grade III, J I Moore and H C Pereira, Aug. 1949). When free of snow this gully can be climbed down without abseiling (III).

      The tower buttress right of the *South-East Gully* may also have been climbed by a Cape Town University party, in January 1965.

2. South Ridge

First ascent: R Merendi, L Marimonti and G Gualco, 17th Jan. 1958.

Standard: IV inf.
Time: Half a day.

From start of *South-East Gully,* traverse left and climb to a white spot on the crest of the South Ridge. Straight up very steep rock to a little gully, the right-hand branch of which leads to the top of the first tower. The next tower is the crux and is taken diagonally from left to right. Two more towers bring one to the right of the summit tooth.

Variation: Instead of starting up the South-East Gully, climb the slab and wall directly beneath the South Ridge. (Grade VI, B Shapiro and G Tabin, February 1980).

During the last few years some very difficult climbing has been done on the vertical western and northern faces of Point John. The following four routes, in particular, should be considered as major undertakings.

3. **South-West Face**
First ascent: I F Howell and I J Allan, 17th, 18th and 19th July, 1977.
Standard: A3.
Time: 3 days.

The steepest section of this face is on the right side where a prominent dihedral leads up leftwards to an obvious corner. Three long pitches lead to this corner. Another long pitch then goes up the corner to bulges, which are taken on the left, then straight up to steep slabs. (Hanging Bivouac Site). Up slightly right to foot of chimney, which is climbed to a break leading leftwards to a down-sloping ramp. At the foot of this a thin crack is climbed to a ledge. This is the first ledge on the climb and marks the end of the aid climbing. Easier pitches (III) lead up to the South Ridge.

A good selection of nuts from small wire to the biggest sizes, plus blade pegs and small angles. Hammocks are useful for the first bivouac.

4. *West Face*

First ascent: P Plachecky and Z Drlik, 12th ,13th and 14th Jan., 1980.

Standard: V sup., A4.

Time: 3 days.

Scramble up slabs to a point half-way between the start of the *South-West Face Route and the North-West Arete Route*. Two long pitches follow crack line to a belay on the Black Tower. Three further pitches above joins the North-West Arete Route, which comes in from the left. Trend right for two pitches before going more directly to the summit.

5. **North-West Arete**

First ascent: R W Baillie and T Phillips, March 1964.

Standard: VI, A2

Time: 3 days.

From the notch between Point John and Midget Peak a prominent pillar leans against the wall. Climb to the top of this (VI). From this point 10 pitches of A1 and A2 lead up the wall to the summit. There are no real stances.

6. **North Face**

First ascent: P Plachecky and Z Drlik, 17th, 18th and 19th Jan., 1980.

Standard: V sup, A4.

Time: 3 days

The route starts at the lowest point of the North Face below big ledges, a quarter of the way up the face. Reach the big ledges in two pitches by a crack line just right of the most obvious V-groove. Above the ledges the middle corner is climbed for a pitch and a half, where you move right and up to the line of overhangs. These are taken on aid either left (A2), or right (A4). The middle corner is followed for two pitches to ledges right of a yellow slab. Climb left-hand corner and continue almost directly to the summit.

7. Quo Vadis

First ascent: P Plachecky (solo), 2nd and 3rd Feb., 1980.
Standard: VI.
Time: 12 hours.

Start just right of the foot of the Point John Couloir. After some 30 m move right into a groove, and continue for another 65 m to a ledge on right. Two short hard grooves lead to a 6 m chimney. Up this with difficulty to belay above. Hard climbing continues to a V-groove above the left end of the line of overhangs. Up this and continue to a flake on the left. Aim for a ledge below a smooth triangular wall. Ascend its left edge to a ledge below on top of it. Groove lead in two pitches to the summit ridge.

8. Point John Couloir

First ascent: P Snyder, D Karinga, T Mathenge and S Gitonga, May 1972.
Standard: V.
Time: Half a day.

This couloir, which is very seasonal, can be reached most easily from Two Tarn Hut It is situated between the North Face of Point John and the West Face of the ridge linking Point John with Nelion. Start at foot of obvious ice couloir. The couloir is climbed in about four pitches.

Point John Minor is the prominent spire which forms the northern peak of point John. From it, the main ridge of the main peak can be reached. Two routes have been climbed on this spire.

1. *Original Route*

First ascent: H Graffland and J P Schoon, 10th July, 1958.
Standard: IV.
Time: Half a day.

Start from the notch connecting Point John with the South Ridge of Nelion, and climb the North Face via two cracks.

2. South-East Ridge

First ascent: G Ward, A Manhire, and G Moseley, January 1965.

Standard: V.

Time: Half a day.

Start up a face with a crack (pitch 1), then traverse right and up a crack. These pitches are the hardest on the climb. The route now continues up over a knife-edge ridge, over several gendarmes to Point John Minor.

Shipton, Tilman, Grigg & Sommerfelt Peaks and Castle hill are all readily accessible from Top Hut. They provide good ridge walking and the peaks are easy scrambles.

Coryndon, Delamere & Mcmillan Peaks have been unjustly neglected, possibly because of their reputation (not entirely merited) for unsound rock. Two routes have been recorded on Delamere Peak.

1. South-East Face of Delamere Peak

First ascent: P. Sellers and I. McMorrin, 20th Jan 1960.

Standard: III.

Continue over the col between Delamere Peak and the ridge leading to Coryndon Peak, until slightly right of the summit. Climb diagonally left until a col is reached on the main ridge, which is then followed to the summit.

2. North Face of Delamere Peak

First ascent: J. R. King and M. F. Baker, 26th Dec. 1971.

Standard: II.

Time: 2 hours,

This Climb starts from the col immediately to the right of Delamere Peak when viewed from Hall Tarns Hut. It can be easily reached from this hut in about two hours, by ascending the Gorges Valley until opposite Hanging Tarn, and then climbing up to gain the col. From the col ascend leftwards onto the northern face, whence about 150 m of climbing on snow and rock lead slightly to the left of the main summit.

The Hat (or The Pillar) is reached from the Austrian Hut via the Gorges Valley, but it is also accessible from the Hinde Valley. It can be climbed from the north in little more than a scramble. The other faces are very steep and exposed, and in places they overhang just below the summit.

CLIMBS FROM TWO TARN HUT

From Two Tarn Hut *Arthur's Seat* (4,666 m), is a short scramble from the col between it and Point pigott. There is one worthy technical route up the steep southern face:

Styx
First ascent: P. Snyder and D. Karinga, Jan. 1974.
Standard: VI.
Time: 8 hours.
Start at cairn at the foot of an obvious dihedral. Up the steep crack to a niche and the cave above. Turn the over-hand on the left wall (crux), onto a steep slab. Up the chimney passing a chockstone, to a widening gully. Left up a ramp then step right to the main gully and a cave. Left onto slabs and easier ground.

Point Pigott (4,957 m), is the fourth highest peak on the mountain and commands fine views from its summit. There is a scrambling route up it from the *Tyndall Glacier* to the summit ridge, using a broad gully. The ridge to the summit is easy by exposed and a rope should be used. Other fine routes exist on this peak:

1. **North-West Face**
First ascent: E. Shipton and H. W. Tilman, 6th Aug. 1930.
Standard: III

Time: Half a day.

Start at the ridge which connect Point Pigott with Arthur's Seat. At the top of the ridge descend over a flake on the north side to a platform by the *Window* (clearly visible from Two Tarn Hut). A sensational step-across is made to a crack in the main face leading up to the left. Climb crack until steep but climbable rock is reached; then traverse left along an easy ledge to *Yellow Gully*. Descend into the gully, cross it and climb up the centre of the left part of the face. A narrow ridge leads to the summit. If this route is used for descent a hanging rope should be left to facilitate re-ascent of the flake by the Window.

2. South Ridge

First ascent: W M and R J H Chambers, Feb. 1959.
Standard: III sup, with one pitch of V if Second Tower is climbed.
Time: 6 hours.

From Two Tarn Hut pass the eastern end of the tarn and walk straight up to the foot of the ridge. The first tower yields to a scramble. The *Second Tower* is the crux. Climb the right-hand gully until a difficult breakout can be made to a ledge on the left skyline. Climb the steep groove a few feet right of the ridge. Surmount a slight overhang at 15 m from belay and reach a stance at a large block 9 m higher up and to the left. A second, easier pitch reaches the top of the Tower. This Tower can be by-passed by a simple traverse to the left across onto the West Face; an easy gully then meets the ridge above the difficulties. The route continues along the ridge to the summit.

3. South Face

First ascent: D. J. Temple and L. Smith, Jan. 1975.
Standard: V
Time: Half a day.

Scramble to a small amphitheatre directly below the summit, then up a gully to the left for a pitch, when it is possi-

to traverse right above the overhang. A steep climb to a niche, then right onto an edge and up slabs to the top.

4. East-North-East ridge
First ascent: A B Clark and R W Baillie, 19th Dec. 1960.
Standard: V.
Time: 3 hours from Firmin Col.

From *Tyndall Glacier* climb the steep gully leading to Firmin Col. Instead of climbing all the way to col, move left and reach the ridge above the col. Follow ridge to summit overcoming two towers.

5. West Face
First ascent: Cape Town University party, 1965.
Standard: IV.
Time: Half a day.

Start the climb at the highest point of the scree at the broken rock to the right of the very steep walls below the summit. The route trends generally left towards the summit.

6. Tyndall Buttress
First ascent: I. F. Howell and D. J. Temple, March 1975.
Standard: V
Time: Half a day.

To the right of the scrambling route gully, is an ill-defined ridge ending at a steep tower which is climbed by a chimney crack system.

Midget Peak (4,700 m), offer some fine routes on good rock. The easiest descent is by climbing a little way down towards the col between Point John and Midget Peak, and making one long abseil.

1. *South Gully*
First ascent: E. E. Shipton and H. W. Tilman, 9th Aug. 1930.
Standard: IV.

Time: Half a day.

This is the main gully on the South Face of Midget. The first 25 m climbs an awkward crack, then a 20 m scramble is made. A 25 m pitch follows; then a series of short pitches of columnar rock. 5 m of loose rock lead to a 9 m wall ending in a small cave. Up the left wall to wide recess. Climb right-hand wall of recess, then leftwards on narrow, outward-sloping ledge to a wide ledge. Traverse left on exposed sloping ledges and climb bulge. A 6 m crack leads to a 9 m pitch up a sloping slab, which leads round onto the north side. An awkward corner leads to a vertical crack at the top of which is small platform. Scramble over ridge and down left to a steep crack, at the top of which is another platform. From here a short climb round an exposed nose to the left then up to summit.

Variation: The middle section has been by-passed on the left, (R A Caukwell and Miss A Rowe, 1st Feb. 1952).

2. **South-South-West Buttress**
First ascent: Cape Town University party, 5th Jan. 1965.
Standard: IV sup.
Time: Half a day.

Climb the buttress between the South and South-West Gullies on the front, and then move on to the wall above the South Gully to reach the summit of *Midget Minimus*, the top of the pillar.

3. **South-West Gully**
First ascent: G. Low and D. Bell, 31st Jan. 1952.
Standard: III sup.
Time: Half a day.

This is the gully (very obvious from Two Tarn Hut), which is situated between Midget Peak and Midget Minor. From foot of gully climb for 27 m to the top of left-hand crack. Scramble for 30 m to where it steepens. Climb wall then traverse to a central crack leading to big ledge. Follow ledge right to another ledge. Climb the crack on the left, sloping upwards from right to left; this is climbed for 3 m to a niche. Out left and traverse for 9 m on sloping ledge to large ledge. A wide recess on the left lead to easy-angled Slab. From here join *South Gully Route* at the easy sloping slab which leads to north side and follow that route to summit.

4. **West Face**
First ascent: I D Sandilands and I F Howell, Jan. 1969.
Standard: V, A2.
Time: Half a day.
      Near the bottom of the steep face of Midget, facing Two Tarn Hut is an orange pyramidal steep slab with a thin crack running up it. Climb to ledge below crack. Traverse right to chimney; ascend this to belay. Ascend to square chimney (pendule into bottom), then traverse across slab left, and up to a ledge below little corner. Climb this to large blocks, and ascend broken groove above to final overhang. Traverse left slightly down until one can ascend again to flake and ledge. Move right to little crest with short steep wall. Climb this to easy ground leading to summit. This route consists of mixed aid and free climbing.

5. **Nek Pad**
First ascent: R W Baillie, W M Boyes and C Rhys-Jones, 6th Jan. 1961.
Standard: IV.
Time: Half a day.
      Start on col between Midget and Point John. Climb steep slab sloping up right to small stance. Straight up for 20 m over bulge to another stance. Traverse right and up 3 m wall. Traverse right again across 3 m "lip" onto a rib, and climb this. Climb crack above small col.

6. **Nek-Line**
First ascent: G. B. Cliff and R. Smith, 19th Jan 1962.

Standard: V, A1.

Time: Half a day.

From the col *(nek)* between Point John and Midget ascend ridge, and after 15 m step round corner onto North Face. Up shallow groove to a pile of loose boulders in a corner. Traverse right round the corner and ascend 41/2 m to recess. From here a fine crack runs up to right-hand corner (3 aid moves). Continue up groove to top.

7. North Face

First ascent: Y Chouinard and E Deahl, 29th Jan 1975.

Standard: VI.

Time: Half a day.

Follow the crack system leading directly to summit. A good line, with the crux being the first pitch.

8. South-East Buttress

First ascent: R J H Chambers and M C P Moore, 21st Jan. 1966.

Standard: V inf.

Time: Half a day.

Start at the foot of a sheer reddish face immediately right of the South Gully. Scramble round base of face and up to a platform at the foot of obvious corner which leads onto the ridge of the buttress. Up corner for 50 m to ridge, avoiding overhanging chockstone on the right wall. Up ridge with a small overhang at 15 m (crux), Up groove above and two subsequent problems can be turned by a short traverse left, and by moving a few metres right respectively.

9. Midget Minor

First ascent: W M Adams and R J H Chambers, 5th Feb. 1959.

Standard: IV sup.

Time: Half hour from col between two Midget Peaks.

From the notch traverse the slab left for 15 m to a stance. Easy rocks now lead to summit.

10. Midget Minimus
First ascent: D. Berrisford and G. War, 5th Jan. 1965.
Standard: V.
Time: Half a day.
       Start at the left-hand side of the South Gully, and scramble up an easy recess which leads to large stance. Climb 25 m straight up to a lichen-covered face, and then climb 20 m slightly to the left towards recess with jammed blocks Up these stance, then take the lower traverse level rightwards for 25 m. Climb corner and traverse right to chockstone-filled crack. Up 20 m to ramp. Up ramp and above to summit of Minimus. From here the summit of Midget Peak can be reached by joining either the South Gully or the South-West Gully.

11. Nek-Lace
First ascent: P. Snyder and I. Cunningham, 5th March 1973.
Standard: V.
Time: Half a day.
       From the upper part of Nek Pad, traverse right to the notch below the summit on the side. Descend ramp on the west side and continue the traverse about 15 m below the top.

POINT SLADE (4,750 m)
       This is the summit of the buttress on the eastern side of the South-West Couloir of Batian. There is an easy descent from the col between Point Slade and the South-West Ridge of Batian. Several routes have been climbed on Point Slade:

1. South Face
First ascent: I. F. Howell and D. J. Temple, March 1974.
Standard: V sup.
Time: Half a day.

Start from the lowest of a series of corners slanting leftwards up the face. From the col at the top traverse left to the foot of a step wall, which is climbed by a difficult crack (crux). Move right into corner, and up this to follow ridge to summit.

2. The Great Slab
First ascent: I. J. Allan and I. F. Howell 3rd Feb. 1975.
Standard: V.
Time: Half a day.
The second and largest corner is reached in four hard pitches. Easily up slab to the upper section of the *South Face Route.*

3. Speaker's Corner
First ascent: D. J. Temple and R. Gocking, 3rd Feb. 1975.
Standard: V.
Time: Half a day.
Start on broken rock directly below the Great Slab. The second and third pitches, a steep corner and a traverse right are hard. Cross the Great Slab near its base and work up an interesting series of corners to top.

4. East Rib
First ascent: D. J. Temple and I. F. Howell, 8th March 1975.
Standard: V.
Time: Half a day.
Easily up ice-worn slabs to a chimney with steeper sections above.
It should be noted that the Point John Couloir is more easily reached from Two Tarn Hut. See under routes on Point John.

CLIMBS FROM KAMI HUT

Point Dutton (4,885 m). The peak can be ascended by an

easy route which is mostly scrambling. However, there is some Grade II climbing on the ridge between the top of the north gully and the summit. The Kami Hut Book contains an entry stating that the Lyon section of the C.A.F. climbed Point Dutton by the *"Arete du Gendarme"*. This was probably the right-hand ridge of the North-East Face. The route below takes a line up the centre of this face.

NORTH-EAST FACE AND RIDGE
First ascent: S. Barusso and R. D. Metcalfe, 4th Aug. 1966.
Standard: IV.
Time: Half a day.
   From the lowest point of the crag facing Kami Hut scramble up about 30 m to a large platform. From here a deep chimney runs up the centre of face. Up slabs on left for 25 m then enter chimney above large block (III). Up 15 m then follow gangway left for 3 m until ledge above can be reached. Up gully above to platform. Enter overhung groove on left via detached flake (IV), and cross to small pinnacle; 5 m of traversing to the left leads to the foot of Y-shaped groove. The left-hand branch is taken for 12 m (IV), then easier climbing trends to the right to the foot of the pinnacle which marks the foot of the North-East Ridge. Up ridge to summit.

POINT PETER (4,757 m), the sharp spire overlooking the Hausburg col has some fine routes. Descent from the summit is made by one abseil down into the North-East Gully, followed by scrambling.

1. North-East Gully and Ridge
First ascent: E. E. Shipton and H. W. Tilman, July 1930.
Standard: III.
Time: Half a day.
   An obvious gully leads to the North-East Ridge. Then rope down to another gully which leads to the summit.

2. **Window Ridge**

First ascent: F. A. Wedgewood and H. G. Nicol, 8th Aug. 1963.
Standard: VI, AI.
Time: Three-quarters of a day.

This is the righthand skyline ridge as seen from Kami Hut. Start at the col between the big gendarme and the ridge, the Window being above here. Easy climbing up the ridge; then where the ridge steepens just above the Window, climb the crack for 8 m (V) and descend into notch. Up ridge steeply for 30 m (V), then traverse left 12 m to foot of diedre. Up this (VI, AI), then break out right and climb slab for 9 m (IV). Easily to summit.
Note: This route is now usually climbed free at grade VI.

3. **East Face Corner and North-East Ridge**

First ascent: R. J. H. Chambers, P. Gerrard and M. Harris, July 1967.
Standard: IV sup.
Time: Half a day.

This route takes the yellow face as seen from Kami Hut, via obvious slanting grooves. Start at the base of a prominent corner groove just right of the smoothy yellow wall. Climb the broken corner to large ledge at 75 m. Continue in same line to platform.

Do not go up groove, but traverse 5 m to the right and up a steep wall to niche; continue up blocks to another niche at the base of another groove. Up this slanting chimney, breaking out at top on to left wall for final 8 m. Stance on ridge. Up ridge to pinnacle and descend 3 m to the col at the top of *Shipton-Tilman Gully*. Descend 7 m and cross to corner, up this to hand-traverse leading into groove, then up some good cracks to a large block. Up ridge to summit.

4. **South Ridge.**

First ascent: R. J. H. Chambers and M. Harris, 21st July 1967.
Standard: IV.
Time: 3 hours.

This is the left-hand skyline ridge seen from Kami Hut. Start at base of ridge by col. Climb up on the prow for 25 m then up and traverse right across some detached blocks. Move up and left to a large platform on the ridge; layback up until under the overhang; move right and up a steep wall and then to the ridge.

Follow this to summit.

5. **West Ridge**
First ascent: E. Drushke and P. Anderson, July 1975.
Standard: V sup, A1.
Time: Half a day.

Avoid the vertical buttress at the base of the ridge by a series of ledges on the right. Reach the ridge and follow it to where it steepens. Move right and climb steep crack. Briefly regain crest then right to a corner and climb cracks (A1). Above work left to skyline and then summit.

Point Lenana may be reached from Kami Hut by contouring below the base of the North Ridge of Batian, then ascending the lateral moraine of the Gregory Glacier to Harris Tarn. See under " Climbs from Austrian Hut".

Point Pigott. *The East-North-East Ridge route* (from Firmin Col) is also accessible from Kami Hut, and this route is described under "Climbs From Two Tarn Hut".

CLIMBS FROM LIKI NORTH HUT

Tereri (4,714 m) and Sendeyo (4,704 m)
First ascent: E. E. Shipton and H. W. Tilman, 5th Aug. 1930.

There is some doubt which of the peaks this party climbed. Although Shipton wrote shortly after that they had climbed Sendeyo from Flake Col, he later believed it was probably Tereri, the higher peak, which they climbed. He originally described their route as 'not interesting except for the view, although the peak has a very fine appearance". In August, 1931, Humphrey J Slade scrambled solo up Sendeyo, and this may have been the first ascent of the lower peak.

Tereri is easily climbed from Liki North Hut and Valley by its North-West or its North-East ridge. The upper part of the latter route may also be reached from the Mackinder Valley by climbing to the col between Tereri and Sendeyo, then descending not more than 30 m on the north side; the rock does not exceed Grade II.

Sendeyo may also be climbed from the col to the west, and West Face has been descended.
          These peaks afford fine views of the North Face of Batian and Nelion, and a traverse of the two peaks from east to west would form a good outing. Care must be taken as the rock is none too sound in places. There is scope for exploration from the north, and interested parties will find a convenient campsite due north of Sendeyo in the area of the 4,400 m col between the heads of the Liki North and Sirimon valleys.

There are records of four climbing routes on these two peaks:

1. South Face of Tereri
First ascent: W. M. Adams and R. J. H. Chambers, 25th Jan. 1959.
Standard: III.
Time: 2 hours from foot of gully to summit
          A prominent gallery runs across the South Face just below the level of the col. Traverse along this until right below and close in to the main mass of the peak. On the right there is a deep, narrow gully formed by a shattered dyke. Follow this gully (normally an ice-couloir), until about two-thirds up, a break out left can be made. Moving leftwards another gully is reached and followed to summit.

2. **West-North-West Ridge of Tereri.**

First ascent: F. A. Wedgewood, H. G. Nicol and S. Wedgewood, 5th Aug. 1963.

Standard: V.

Time: 2 hours from col to summit.

This is the skyline ridge of Tereri as seen from Mackinder Valley in the region of Shipton's Cave, and should not be confused with the easier North-West Ridge which drops into the Liki North Valley. Start from the col immediately west of the prominent Finger which can be seen from Mackinder valley. Climb on the north side of up a chimney to the notch behind the Finger. Two short pitches (III) follow, then easy scrambling for about 60 m. A steep band of red rock must be climbed. Climb easily to foot of Band then traverse left and climb a 9 m chimney (V). A 9 m pitch (IV) is followed by easy climbing to summit.

3. **South-East Chimney of Sendeyo**

First ascent: J. W. Howard and O. Gabrioli, 6th Feb. 1945.

Standard: III.

Time: 2 hours.

The complex of chimneys at the south end of the South end of the South-East Face, immediately above the point where the ridge defining the Hinde Valley watershed joins the face. The route generally follows the right-hand chimneys, which lead directly to summit.

4. **North-East Ridge of Sendeyo**

First ascent: W. M. Adams and R. J. H. Chambers, 25th Jan. 1959.

Standard: IV.

Time: 21/2 hours.

There is prominent aiguille at the base of the East Ridge. The route onto the ridge lies in the gully directly next to this on the peak side. Ascend ridge turning all difficulties on the south side. From the fore-summit, an awkward descent brings one to easy ridge and summit.

OUTLYING CLIMBS

Castle Rock
First ascent: B. Davis and R. Parker, February 1970.
Standard: IV.
  The rock is easily identified as the prominent tower on the south side of the Teleki Valley, opposite the site of the now demolished Klarwills Hut. Three cracks go up the right side. Scramble 15 m up left chimney to large chockstone. Another 4 m to ledge then right 3 m into alcove. Move left into final gully.

Ricochette
First ascent: P. Snyder and I. F. Howell, 16th Aug. 1971.
Standard: VI.
  This climb ascends the cliffs at the head of the Upper Nithi Gorge, directly beneath Hall Tarns. The cliff is about 200 m high, and its base may be reached in half an hour from Minto's Hut. Start at the narrowest point of the Gorge, and the most obvious line up a groove is taken. This ends at the foot of the final wall, which is climbed by means of a 60 m steep over-hanging chimney on the left. Six pitches were climbed.

WALK ROUND THE PEAKS

The walk round the peaks reveals a remarkable variety of fine mountain scenery, and may be accomplished in one day. Many people will, however, prefer to do this trip in a more leisurely fashion, walking during the best of the early morning weather and stopping for the afternoon and night in one of the huts. The route is here described in three sections starting from Austrian Hut, but of course, a start may be made from any of the three huts.
Austrian Hut to Kami Hut.
  The shortest route is up the Lewis Glacier, over the col immediately east of Point Thomson, and down a very steep snow slope onto the Gregory Glacier. Then contour below the

base of the North Ridge of Batian to Kami Hut. This route can be done in about 2 1/2 hours, but it is only recommended for roped parties with experience of snow and ice. Crampons are necessary.

Other parties should go from Austrian Hut to Square Tarn and up to Simba Col. A short distance over the col traverse left and cross the lateral moraine of the Gregory Glacier, and join the other route below the base of Batian's North Ridge (4 hours).

Kami Hut to Two Tarn Hut

From Kami Hut climb to Hausburg Col (north of Point Peter), and descend the other side to Oblong Tarn. Skirt to the left of the tarn and climb to the 4,640 m col between Arthur's Seat and Point Pigott, from where there is an easy descent to Two Tarn Hut (3 1/2 hours).

Alternatively, and more commonly, go between Oblong and Hausburg Tarn and then either (I) up to the col between Western Terminal and Arthur's Seat at 4,500 m or (II) round the base of Western Terminal and climb to join (I) below the cliffs of Arthur's Seat. From here contour to Two Tarn Hut.

Two Tarn Hut to Austrian Hut

There is no need to descend as low as the mule route described under the Burguret Route. The stream from the Lewis Glacier can be crossed at about 4,450 m, and from here the lateral moraine can be reached to join the normal route to Austrian Hut (2 1/2 hours).

Alternatively descend 60 m from Hut Tarn and contour round to the base of Midget Peak. Then mount to the base of Point John and eventually, cross the Lewis Glacier to the Curling Pond.

HISTORY OF CLIMBING ON MT. KENYA

The three great snow masses of East Africa - Kilimanjaro (5,895 m), Kenya (5,199 m), and Ruwenzori (5,110 m) - were first seen by Europeans in that order. That is, in order of nearness to the coast, which happens also to be the order of altitude. They were also explored and climbed in the same order - Kibo being first climbed in 1889, Batian in 1899 and Margherita in 1906.

When the C.M.S. missionary Rebmann claimed to have seen the snow-dome of Kibo in 1848, he was laughed at. Similar scorn was poured on his colleague, Dr. Krapf, when he claimed to have seen the glaciers of Mount Kenya from Kitui, nearly 16 km. away, in 1849. Many geographers said that what they had actually seen was the glistening of "calcareous earth", but nothing could shake the conviction of the two missionaries. It was not, however, until 1883 that confirmation of Krapf's claim was received from Joseph Thomson, who passed close to Mount Kenya on his way across the Laikipia Plateau.

Four years later, exploration of the mountain began. It is convenient to divide the account of this into three periods:

a) 1887-1899: First tentative exploration culminating in Mackinder's remarkable ascent of Batian.
b) 1900-1930: Detailed exploration of the moorlands, but no more successful attempts on the peaks until the series of climbs made by E. E. Shipton with other climbers in 1929 and 1930.
c) 1931- to the present day: Consolidation of the results of the previous periods and the pioneering of new climbing routes on the peaks.

1887 - 1899

Count Teleki's expedition of 1887 (von Hohnel 1894) was the first to set foot on the mountain proper. A height of about 4,350 m was reached, well up the moorland zone on the south-western slopes of the mountain.

Two or three years later an official British East Africa Company expedition led by Captain F. G. Dundas made an attempt on the southern slopes, but failed to penetrate the forest belt (Gedge 1892).

In 1893 the geologist Dr. J. W. Gregory arrived in

East Africa as a member of an abortive expedition. Determined, however, not to return to England, without something to show for his journey, he organised an expedition of his own from the coast to the Rift Valley and as far north as Lake Baringo. As the only European in the party - and moreover a man quite unacquainted with the country; and the natives - his achievements were remarkable. Not the least remarkable was his ascent of Mount Kenya to the glacier zone at about 4,730 m. Accompanied by an African named Fundi (who had also been with Teleki), he spent several hours on the Lewis Glacier. On his return to Britain he published papers on the Geology and Glacial Geology of Mount Kenya, in addition to the narrative accounts of his expedition.

In 1896 George Kolb was the first man to reach the moorlands from the east; but it was Mackinder's expedition of 1899 which followed up Gregory's success in a brilliant fashion. H. J. (later Sir Halford) Mackinder is regarded as the pioneer of geography teaching as we know it today. It was his interest in geography as much as in climbing which led him to organise his expedition to Mount Kenya.

In 1899 the railway had just reached the present site of Nairobi, and it was from here that Mackinder's party set out on their long march to the mountain. In those days safaris were, of necessity, organised on a large scale, and his party consisted of "6 Europeans, 66 Swahilis, 2 tall Masai guides, and the remainder (96) naked Wakikuyu". Apart from Mackinder himself, the Europeans were C B Hausburg (second-in-common and photographer), Saunders (botanist), Camburn (taxidermist), Cesar Ollier (guide) and Josef Brocherel (porter). The last two were from Courmayeur.

The approach march through Kikuyu country was beset with many difficulties: the country was plague-ridden and suffering from famine; his kikuyu porters tried to desert, and some of the chiefs through whose territory he tried to pass were very hostile. Trouble continued at base camp, while the climbing party was up the mountain: the porters had great difficulty in obtaining food, and two of them were killed by local natives. Eventually, Saunders had to be sent across difficult and unknown country to obtain help from Captain Gorges, the Government officer at Naivasha.

Inspite of these difficulties the assault on the mountain was pressed forward. Ollier and Brocherel succeeded in cutting a path through the forest in one day, and camp was established at 3,142 m, in the Hohnel Valley (which had also been Gregory's approach to the mountain). Although the porters carried for more than 900 metres above this, crossing into the Teleki Valley, they always returned to this camp at night. Mackinder's first attempt on the peak ended 100-120 m from the summit of Nelion, the party being benighted on the South-East Face. Hausburg next made a complete circuit of the peaks with the two guides, climbing point Lenana on the way, but no easy way up the main peak could be found. Ollier and Brocherel next made an ascent of the Darwin Glacier, but they were forced by a blizzard to descend over the South Ridge of Nelion.

On the return of Saunders from Naivasha with the relief party, Mackinder, determined to make one last attempt on Batian before beating a retreat. With Ollier and Brocherel his route lay across the Lewis Glacier and up the South-East Face of Nelion via the chimney named after him; a bivouac was made near the gendarme. At dawn next day a traverse was made across the snowfield at the head of the Darwin Glacier, over a rocky rib, and then - most difficult of all - three hours of step cutting across the narrow, but extremely hard and steep Diamond Glacier. There remained only a rock scramble, and the summit of Batian was attained for the first time at noon on 13th September, 1899. The descent, by the same route, was made in deteriorating weather conditions, and they did not reach camp at the head of the Teleki Valley until 10 p.m.

Mount Kenya. Climbing the Diamond Couloir Headwall.   Iain Allan

References:

L von Hohnel: *The discovery of Lakes Rudolf and Stefanie* (1894).

E Gedge: *A Recent Exploration, under Capt.. F.G. Dundas, up the River Tana to Mount Kenya* (Proc. Royal Geog. Soc, No. VIII, 1892, p.257).

J W Gregory: *The Great Rift Valley (1896). Contributions to the Physical Geography of British East Africa* (Geog. Journal Vol. IV, 1894, p. 408).

H J Mackinder: *A Journey to the Summit of Mount Kenya, British East Africa* (Geog. Journal Vol. XV, 1900, p. 453).

1900 - 1930

After Mackinder's triumph there was a pause in activity on the mountain. In 1908 the glaciers were visited by Macgregor Ross, and by Kermit Roosevelt; but most of the exploration was done, particularly after the First World War, by Kenya settlers with no scientific pretensions. Of these the most prominent were Rev Dr. J. W. Arthur, G. Dennis, A. R. Barlow (all Church of Scotland missionaries), E. A. T. Dutton (whose charming book is typical of the spirit of those days), J. Melhuish and E. Carr.

The expeditions of these men were too many to describe here in detail. Several unsuccessful attempts were made on the main peaks, but none got further than the South Ridge of Nelion, where even the introduction by Melhuish of a ladder as a climbing aid failed to enable him to cross a wide gap.

Their main achievements, apart from the fact that they really enjoyed the mountain, were a thorough exploration of the moorlands and the making of new approach routes through the forest belt. Arthur, with Sir Fowell Buxton, in 1920 tried a route from the south; routes from Nanyuki were opened up; but the most popular route of those days was probably that from the Chogoria Mission on the eastern slopes. Earnest Carr was mainly responsible for this last route; he not only built the track but was also responsible for the erection of the first two huts on the mountain - Urumandi Hut (3,063 m) and Top Hut (4,790 m), beside the Curling Pond.

This second period ends with four ascents of the two main peaks in 1929 and 1930. On 6th Jan. 1929, P Wyn Harris, then a District Commissioner, and E. E. Shipton, a farm manager, having unsuccessfully attempted the North-East Face of Batian, made the first ascent of Nelion by what is now considered the Normal Route

From the summit of Nelion they descended into the Gate of the Mists and then climbed Batian. Two days later they repeated the ascent with G. A. Sommerfelt making a third on the rope; and in December of that year Shipton again did the climb with R. E. G. Russell.

In July, 1930, Shipton with H. W. Tilman made the long ascent of the West Ridge of Batian. The descent was made over Nelion by the Normal Route, thus completing the first traverse of the mountain. Shipton and Tilman also made the first ascents of Midget Peak, Point Pigott, Point Peter, and either Sendeyo or Tereri. Shipton had previously, with Russell, made the first ascent of Point John.

References:

J W Arthur: *Mount Kenya* (Geog. Journal Vol. LVIII, 1921, p. 8.)

E A T Dutton: *Kenya Mountain* (1939).

E E Shipton: *Upon that Mountain* (1943) and *That Untravelled World*. (1969). Also, articles from the Times and the Alpine Journal reprinted in "The Ice-Cap" No. 1 (1932), the first journal of the Mountain Club of East Africa.

H W Tilman: *Snow on the Equator* (1937).

1931 To The Present Day

Once again achievement was followed by a period of comparative inactivity. Visits to the moorlands were made by Kenya Europeans; Raymond Hook and Humphrey Slade stocked some of the streams with trout and did some valuable mapping.

Batian was not climbed again, as far as records

show, until 1936 when H. J. Irens and E. Sladen made the ascent by the Normal Route. In February 1938 a party of four which climbed Nelion included Miss C. Carrol (the first woman to climb the peak), and Mtu Mathara (the first African). A month later, on 5th March, Batian was climbed by Miss U. Cameron - the first woman to reach the summit of Mount Kenya. She was accompanied by two Courmayeur guides; the next day Miss G. Sladen made the ascent with her brother. It seemed as if interest in the peaks was increasing when the war came.

The most notable incident during the 1939-45 War was the gallant attempt by three Italian prisoners of war to climb the mountain. They failed to make a lodgement on the West Ridge of Batian, and they had to be content with the ascent of Lenana. The account of the improvisation of their equipment, the storing up of their meagre rations, their break-out from the Nanyuki camp, and their route-finding without the assistance of any map make fascinating reading (Benuzzi 1952).

After the War the mountain became increasingly popular with climbers. In 1949 the Mountain Club of Kenya began its existence separate from the Mountain Club of East Africa (which had been formed in 1929). The mountain above 3,400 m became a National Park, and the road built nearly to the moorlands from Naro Moru by the Parks authorities made the mountain more accessible for visits of a week or less. Early in 1948, Two Tarn Hut (4,490 m), was erected by the Mountain Club with money raised by public subscription, and so the western side of the peaks could be reached. Systematic mapping of the mountain was also done by the Colonial Surveys. In December 1957, as part of the programme for the International Geophysical Year, an expedition of Kenya scientists spent six weeks on the mountain doing a glaciological survey.

The most notable climbs of this period were the first ascent of the North Face of Batian by A. H. Firmin and P. Hicks (July 1944); and the first ascent of the South Face by A. H.

Firmin and J. W. Howard (January 1946) - via the South-West Ridge.

By the beginning of the Emergency (Autumn 1952), about 20 parties had ascended Batian over a period of 53 years. The Emergency put a temporary end to climbing on Mount Kenya, which was now designated a closed area. The West Face of Batian was however climbed by R. A. Caukwell and G. W. Rose (January 1955) The first ascent of Batian by an African was made by Kisoi Munyao in January 1959.

The early sixties saw the emergence of hard, technical routes on the eastern faces on Nelion, with the ascents of the North East Pillar Route, climbed by G. B. Cliff and D. Rutowitz (August 1963); and the East Face Route, climbed by H. Klier, A. Aeberli and G. B. Cliff (August 1963). In the early seventies a National Park Mountain Rescue team was formed.

In January 1980, the first ascent of Batian by an all-female rope was accomplished by Miss S. Morris and Miss L. Wayburn.

In recent years much climbing has been done on the peaks, and technical routes of a very serious nature have evolved. Much of the recent pioneering has been in the hands of I. F. Howell, P. Snyder, D. J. Temple and I. J. Allan. Mention should be made o f the first ascent of the Diamond Couloir by P. Snyder and T. Mathenge (Oct. 1973); the Diamond Buttress Original Route by I. F. Howell and D. J. Temple (March 1976); Nelion's Eastern Groove Route and Batian's North Gate Route by I. F. Howell and I. J. Allan (June 1978 and Sept. 1980).

References:

F Benuzzi: *No picnic on Mount Kenya* (1952).

Bulletins of the Mount Club of Kenya(1946 to date).

Gordon Boy, Iain Allan, Clive Ward *Snowcaps on the Equator* 1989.

PLACE-NAMES ON MOUNT KENYA

The name "Kenya" itself is usually taken to be a corruption of he Kikuyu name for the Mountain - *"Kirinyaga"*. There seem to be some doubt about the meaning of this word (possibly "Mountain of Whiteness"). Certainly, the Kikuyu used to regard the mountain as the home of the great god Ngai.

Krapf said that the Wakamba tribe called it *'Kima Ja Kegnia'* meaning "Mountain of Whiteness", and that other tribes had similar names, e.g. *'Kirenia'* in the Embu language. Some authorities however, say that the Wakamba call it *'Kiima' or Kya Nyaa'* (The Hill of the Cock Ostrich), contracted to *'Kiinyaa'*. From a distance the white glaciers contrast with dark rocks; hence, the comparison with the black and white plumage of the male ostrich.

The Masai also had their names for the mountain - *'Ol Donyo Eibor'* (The White Mountain), and *'Ol Donyo Egere'* (The Speckled Mountain). Mackinder believed - on what authority he does not say - that "Kenya" might be a corruption of a Masai word meaning "mists", therefore he named the col between Batian and Nelion "The Gate of the Mists".

PEAKS

The names of the peaks fall into three main group. First those named by Mackinder, on the suggestion of Hinde (the resident officer in Masailand at the time of his visit), after Masai chieftains. *'Batian'* is named after a famous Laibon or Chief Medicine Man, Mbatiany, who died in 1890. *'Nelion'* was his brother, Nelileng. *'Lenana'* or Olonana, son of Mbatiany, was Laibon at the time of Mackinder's expedition. *'Sendeyo'* was the brother and rival of Olonana. *'Tereri'* (strictly with all syllables short), was another Masai headman.

The second group comprises peaks named after climbers and explorers of the mountain. *'Shipton'*, the first conqueror of Nelion, has a rather miserable pimple at the head of Teleki Valley named after him, quite impressive from below, but very diminutive even from the altitude of Austrian Hut. *'Sommerfelt'*, who accompanied Shipton and Wyn Harris on the second ascent of Nelion, and *'Tilman'*, who did many fine climbs with Shipton in 1930, have peaks name after them. *'Point Dutton'* and *'Arthur's Seat'* are named after men who did such to explore the mountain between 1910 and 1930. In passing it is pleasing to note that Arthur Firmin's name has been commemorated in the Col between Point Pigott and the West Ridge of Batian.

In the third group fall the peaks named after well-known Kenya personalities (most of whom never set foot on the mountain). *'Point Pigott'* after the Acting Administrator of Imperial British East Africa at the time of Gregory's expedition; and four peaks on the S.E. slopes - *'Coryndon'*, *'Grigg'*, *'Delamere'* and *'McMillan'* - after two Kenya governors of the 1920s and two early Kenya settlers respectively. *'Point Slade'* is named after Humphrey Slade who was involved in explorations of the moorland zone in the 1930s, and possibly made the first ascent of Sendeyo.

Melhuish and Dutton were responsible for most of the peak names, except the Masai ones. But, for *'Points Peter'* and *'John'*, named after the two leading apostles, the Scottish missionary J. W. Arthur was appropriately responsible. Mackinder named *'Point Thomson'*, which was not named after Joseph Thomson the famous the famous explorer of Masailand, but after another J. Thomson, official photographer of the Royal Geographical Society. Thomson, did a lot to help Mackinder's photographer, Hausburg, who during the expedition took some of the first-ever colour photos (by a process known as the Ives Process).

GLACIERS

These are transient features for a man's fame to be based on. If the names of two explorers of Mount Kenya, A. R. Barlow and J. Melhuish, were only to be remembered by the glaciers named after them, they would be fast approaching

TROPICAL ICE

East Africa's original adventure safari company, specializes in discovering new trails through unspoiled wildernesses, where you will only see game animals and nomadic people. We also lead expeditions up Mount Kenya, through scenery you'd never have imagined existed. If your idea of an African Safari is something a little more stylish and adventurous than the average package tour, contact us:

oblivion. For the *'Barlow'* Glacier has already disappeared from the slopes of Point Pigott, an the *'Melhuish'* Glacier on the southern ridge of Nelion, overlooking the Lewis Glacier, is only a few square metres of ice. The peak next to this almost extinct glacier is called *'Point Melhuish'*.

Scientists seem likely to retain their names longest on the maps of the Mount Kenya glaciers. *'Gregory'*, the first man to reach the glacier (1893), has one of the north-facing glaciers (which he never saw) named after him. He himself named the glaciers on the S.W. slopes after some of his glaciologist heroes - the *'Lewis'* (after Prof. Carvell Lewis, a 19th century American geologist), the *'Darwin'* (after Charles Darwin), the hanging glaciers *'Heim and 'Forel'* (after two Swiss geologists), and the *'Tyndall'* (after the famous physicist and alpinist, author of "Glaciers of the Alps" and the first conqueror of the Weisshorn in 1861). It is interesting to note, by the way, that Gregory in his original Geographical Journal articles (1894) gave the name *'Darwin'* to the glacier we now call *'Tyndall'* and vice versa; but by the time he wrote "The Great Rift Valley" (1896) he had apparently changed his mind. He was not very consistent over the spelling of names either.

It is well known that the *'Diamond'* Glacier was so called by Mackinder on account of its extreme hardness; and it has also been pointed out how appropriate this name is - for it glitters like a jewel set between Batian and Nelion. Mackinder also named the *'Cesar'* and *'Josef'* Glaciers after his two Courmayeur guides, Collier and J Brocherel, who accompanied him on his first ascent of Batian in 1899.

The remaining north-facing glaciers are named *'Krapf'* (after the CMS missionary who was the first white man to see the mountain in 1849); *'Kolb'* (after an explorer of the eastern slopes of the mountain in 1896); and *'Northey'* (after the Governor of Kenya in the early 1920s).

VALLEYS

Gregory named the *'Teleki'* Valley after the first explorer of the mountain, who reached the head of this valley in 1887; the *'Hohnel'* after Lieut. von Hohnel, the surveyor in Count Teleki's expedition, who did not however take part in the trip up the mountain; and the *'Hobley'* after C. W. Hobley, geologist and cartographer on the British East Africa Company's expedition (1891).

'Mackinders' name is commemorated in the chief valley to the north of the peaks, and the *'Hausburg'* Valley was named by Mackinder after his second-in-command (this valley, incidentally, had earlier been named by Gregory the *'Thomson'* after Joseph Thomson, but this name never stuck). Mackinder also named the *'Hinde'* Valley after the Resident in Masailand who gave his party much help and advice, and the *'Gorges'* after Captain (later Brig. Gen.) E. H. Gorges, the District Commissioner at Naivasha who gave Mackinder's expedition invaluable support when they seemed in danger. Those who have seen the river Nithi flowing through the Gates, bordered by towering 300 m. high cliffs, may think the name *'Gorges'* very appropriate; but it seems to be coincidence.

LAKES

The names of many lakes area descriptive (the little visited *'Enchanted Lakes'*, for instance, named by Raymond Hook; or *'Emerald Tarn'* - appropriate only in certain light condition) Others are named after glaciers or valleys or river, such as *'Tyndall'*, *'Teleki'*, and *'Nanyuki'* tarns.

The *Thompson'* whose name was given by Gregory to the tarns in Hobley valley was W. Bird Thompson, a member of Dundas' 1891 expedition on the southern slopes. Mackinder was responsible for naming *'Hall Tarns'* after the District Commissioner at Fort Hall, and *'Lake Michaelson'* after a great friend who showed much interest in the organisation of his expedition. The 'Vivienne Falls', by the way, on the Nithi below Lake Michaelson, take their name for Miss V. de Watteville, the explorer and the author of "Speak to the Earth", who was on the mountain at the same time as Shipton and Harris's first successful climb (1929).

Dutton and Melhuish named some of the other lakes after climbers and explorers of the mountain - *'Harris Tarn'* after P. Wyn Harris, 'Hook Tarn' after Raymond Hook (or possibly his brother Logan), and *'Carr Lakes'* after Ernest Carr, a prominent founder-member of the Mountain Club of East Africa, who built a track and the Urumandi Hut on the eastern slopes and also the first hut at the Curling Pond. When Jack Melhuish discovered this pond in 1919, his companion, the Scottish missionary Dr. Arthur, taught him the sport of curling, and on his next visit Jack Melhuish took some skates up there. Dutton in his book has entrancing description of him skating on the pond one morning, to the amazement and delight of their African servants and porters.

Another story in Dutton's book is of *'Simba Tarn'* where his porters swore they saw a lion in 1924. Dutton was also responsible for naming *'Lake Alice'* after the Duchess of Gloucester, who visited Kenya soon after the lake was discovered in the 1930s. *'Lake Ellis'* took its name from Thomas Scott-Ellis, Lord Howard de Walden, who accompanied Dutton on his first visit to the lake in 1927.

'Polishman's Tarn' is an intriguing name. Apparently, a free Pole at the end of the war made a trip up the mountain and asked Raymond Hook to recommend a good spot from which to photograph the peaks; Hook suggested this viewpoint, and the Pole was well pleased with the choice. Another lake on the northern slopes is named because of the large number of hyraxes in that area, *"Kikami"*, being the Kikuyu name for a hyrax. Finally, regret may be expressed at the passing of one name from the map - *"Gitchini Tarn'*, named by Jack Melhuish after a personal servant who accompanied him on many expeditions. It is now called *'Hanging Tarn'*.

PART THREE

KILIMANJARO

THE GEOLOGY AND VOLCANOLOGY
OF KILIMANJARO

D N Sampson

Introduction

As the highest mountain in Africa and one of the highest volcanoes of the world, Kilimanjaro merits special attention. Early scientific explorers regarded the mountain as extinct, but more recent investigations suggest that it is dormant. Kilimanjaro's volcanic history has extended over a considerable period of time and has resulted in a wide variety of rock-types.

Regional Geological Setting

Kilimanjaro stands just over 80 km east of the eastern branch of the Rift Valley, known as the Gregory Rift. Volcanic activity was associated with the Rift Valley in late geological times, and considerable areas of lavas were poured out, and large numbers of individual and composite volcanic cones were built up, the deep fractures in the earth's crust providing the channels and lines of weakness that the magma followed. Kilimanjaro is situated at the intersection of major tectonic lines which are apparent along the North Pare Mountains and Lelatema Escarpment to the south, and the lines of major volcanic cones (including Meru, Monduli and Esimingor), to the west.

History of Research

Early investigations of Kilimanjaro were more geographical than geological in nature. The works of Meyer (1900), Jaeger (1909) and Klute (1920), however, include much geological data but, because of difficulties of language, are not widely known in East Africa.

Following the Klute expedition of 1912, few geological observations were recorded until the discovery of sulphur and fumarolic activity in the crater of Kibo by H. W. Tilman in 1933. Tilman's discovery was not confirmed until 1942 when A. H. Firmin of the Mountain Club of Kenya photographed these features. J. J. Richard (1945) and P. C. Spink (1944) carried out several investigations of the Inner Crater and described the fumarolic activity. The first Geological Survey visit to Kibo Crater was not made until 1950. This was followed by a reconnaissance of the Inner Crater in 1951 and a detailed investigation of the sulphur deposits in 1952 (Guest and Sampson, 1952), which led to the investigation by the Sheffield University Expedition 1953, a joint undertaking with the Tanganyika Government (Wilcockson, 1956). Sheffield University was able to send a second expedition in 1957 in connection with the International Geophysical Year.

Description of the Geology

The base of Kilimanjaro measures about 80 x 40 km, elongated in an ESE direction. It consists of three major volcanic centres, Kibo (5,895 m) in the centre; Mawenzi (5,149 m) in the east; an Shira (4,006 m) in the west. There are also many smaller parasitic cones which fall within well-defined belts.

Of the three main centres, little is known of the earlier phases of their activity because later material blankets the preceding stages. It would appear, however, that Shira was the first to become inactive, followed by Mawenzi and finally Kibo.

Shira

The Shira volcano has been considerably eroded, and only the western and southern rims remain. The north and east sides of the collapsed crater or caldera are covered by later material from Kibo. The cone probably reached to over 4,900 m before it collapsed to form a caldera, which was probably about 3 km in diameter. The ring fractures associated with this collapse provided means of outlet for later lavas which welled out onto the caldera floor. Through these lavas an inner core of doleritic agglomerates was extruded which in turn has been intruded by dolerites and basic rocks. The most prevalent rock-type on the Shira Ridge is trachybasalt, characterised by abundant plates of feldspar and consisting of two series separated by ultrabasic lavas (cf. limburgites), which contain olivine and abundant augite phenocrysts. Towards the south-eastern part of the caldera rim, trachybasaltic lava-breccia becomes more abundant. The Shira Ridge exposes a well-developed radial dyke-swarm centred on and cutting the inner core forming the Platz Kegel. These dykes are trachydoleritic, reassembling the trachybasalts in appearance.

Mawenzi

Mawenzi is the most spectacular of the three centres. The western side, which is the one normally seen, is steep for its upper 600 m containing many crags and pinnacles. The East Face, however, is much more impressive, and is cut by two tremendous gorges. It is precipitous for about 1,200 m and is a complex of gullies and rock-faces only partially explored. Klute considered that the precipitous East Face was the result of an explosion which had breached or blown away the eastern crater-rim, in a manner similar to Meru; but more recent investigations suggest that erosion has played the dominant part in the production of this magnificent piece of mountain scenery.

The rocks of Mawenzi closely resemble many of those on Shira. The dominant rock-type on the slopes below the crags is trachybasalt, containing elongate, tabular, plagioclase feldspars and small phenocrysts of yellow olivine and black augite. Inserted inbetween these lavas are olivine basalts, particularly on the southern and south-eastern flanks. These olivine basalts are dark rocks and lack the conspicuous white or pale tabular feldspars. The upper part of the mountain was originally thought to consist of pyroclastic material. It is now considered that, whereas some of the material is agglomerate or tuff, it is mixed with flowbreccia, formed from gassy trachybasaltic lava, and subordinate amounts of solid lava.

One of the most spectacular features of Mawenzi is the intense dyke-swarm. The dykes vary from about 30-180 cm in width, usually about 60-90 cm. The swarm runs ESE; but there are many others which are both radial and concentric to the vent.

On the East Face, C. Dowine and P. Wilkinson of Sheffield University, climbing with A. H. Firmin in 1953, found two plugs of syenite, the larger with a major diameter of about 90 m.

Kibo

By its more perfectly preserved shape and the super-position of it lavas, Kibo is considered to be the most recent of the three centres. The upper part of the mountain still retains its conical shape, but the crater has collapsed to form a caldera 21/2km. in diameter, with inner walls reaching 180 m deep on the southern side. An Inner Cone, rising to within 60 m of the summit height, and over 150 m higher than Gillman's Point, is situated eccentrically within the caldera. This cone is punctured by the Inner Reusch Crater, 820 m in diameter, with-in which is a minor cone, the Ash Cone, with a central crater, the Ash Pit 340 m in diameter and 130 m deep.

The rock-types on upper Kibo show a gradational change from trachybasalt to nephelinite. The earlier lavas are trachybasalts very similar to those on Mawenzi and Shira. These were followed by rocks which have been termed rectangle porphyry, in which the feldspars are more tabular and rectangular in cross-section. These in turn were succeeded by porphyry, in which the feldspar are more tabular and rectangular in cross-section. These in turn were succeeded by rhomb porphyry in which the feldspars are anorthoclase and have rhombic cross-section up to 25 mm across. On the southern and north-western flanks there are considerable areas of phonolite which may have been extruded along fissures. On the caldera rim and in several trains down the slopes, particularly

Mount Kilimanjaro. The Reusch Crater of Kibo.   *David Keith Jones*

on the east and Northeast, there are later lavas which have very conspicuous rhombs of feldspar and contain nephline in addition. Finally the rocks forming the cone and in the Ash Pit, constituting the material inside the caldera, are nephelinites and nepheline phonolites with glassy nepheline phenocrysts, and some pyroxene phenocrysts in a dark, glassy or micro-crystalline matrix. These lavas have filled the caldera and over-flowed down the flanks, particularly in the north-eastern quad-rant where flows extend to below 3,700 m. Smaller flow occurred on the west, and one followed the Western Breach and the valley of the Weru-Weru.

An intrusive body of feldspathoidal syenite is exposed in the Western Breach. It forms conspicuous cliffs encircling the Breach about 600 m below the Notch and extending for nearly a kilometre. It is over 150 m thick and has marked sys-tem of horizontal jointing which gives a layered appearance to the intrusion.

Parasitic Cones

The parasitic cones tend to occur in groups or zones, the most prominent being the Rhombo Zone.

This extends from near Taveta, including the cone and crater at Lake Chala, and continues up the flanks of the mountain in a line with the Ash Pit on Kibo, demarcated by the cones of Oriwo, Maundi Crater, Kifinika, and those on the south side of The Saddle. The materials in these cones are mainly ash and cinder, but some have lava flows which are mainly basalts with olivine and augite phenocrysts. In The Saddle area some of the lavas are ultrabasic, and on the Camel's Back, limburgite lavas with a dyke-feeder are exposed.

Continuing to the Northwest of Kibo is the Lent Group and the North Shira Zone. A little north of this on the lower flanks of the mountain, another zone extends from Ol Molog to the neighbourhood of Sinya. A prominent line of the ash, cinder an lava cones occurs east of Moshi and forms the Kilema-Himo ridge. A less well marked zone runs from Lolgaria to Loosoito in the northeastern foothills.

Description of Volcanology

The younger age of Kibo as compared with Mawenzi and Shira is readily apparent. What is not so certain is the age-relationship of the latter two volcanic centres. It is possible, particularly considering their major rock-types, that Mawenzi and Shira were in part contemporaneous; we must therefore envisage activity at these two centres building up cones to a height of 4,900-5,200 m. At this stage there may have been activity from a central vent under Kibo, but evidence of this is blanked by later volcanic material. The collapse of the Shira cone to form a Caldera was associated with further activity, but Mawenzi does not appear to have suffered a similar collapse. Both centres were heavily intruded by dykes at late stages in their volcanic history.

Although there is a Chagga legend described by Reusch (1936), of Mawenzi borrowing fire for his pipe from his younger brother Kibo, which possibly indicates that some activity has occurred on Mawenzi since the last stage of the Ice Age, there is little geological evidence to support this.

The activity on Kibo can be traced a little more fully and consists of four main phases:
1) the building up of the base cone by trachybasalts and rectangle porphyries
2) the phonolitic fissure eruptions
3) the construction of the upper cone by the rhomb porphyry lavas
4) the filling-in of the caldera by the nepheline rocks of the inner cone and crater.

The lavas of the last two phases were extruded as pahoehoe-type flows which form long narrow tongues down the slopes of the upper cone of Kibo. Some of the parasitic cones appear to have been concurrent with the later phases.

It is not possible to state the ages of these various stages of activity in terms of years. One can, however, confidently state that a considerable amount of activity on Kibo took place during the Pleistocene period. It is possible that the last major episode of activity was within the last few centuries.

As regards the fumarolic activity, first discovered by Tilman in August 1933, it is surprising that subsequent visitors in September and October of the same year, examining the inner crater with the express purpose, failed to confirm his finds. To any visitor to the inner crater since 1950 it is inconceivable that the fumaroles and sulphur deposits could be overlooked. Firmin, on a visit with the writer in 1954, remarked on the increase in conspicuousness of these features since his first visit in 1942. Fumaroles on the northern side of the crater floor, now readily visible, were not noted by either Firmin, Spink or Richard in period 1942-45. It would appear therefore, that there has been some spread of fumarolic activity since it was first noted. An interesting sidelight is the occurrence of plants in the vicinity of some of the mouths of the fumaroles where the increase in temperature brings about localised amelioration of the otherwise arctic conditions. Plants were first noted by the writer in 1952 and on a subsequent visit in 1954 the numbers of both plants and localities were seen to have increased.

The increase of fumarolic activity in the crater is not in itself cause for alarm. Fumaroles may represent the last phase of period of activity. The Sheffield University Kilimanjaro Expedition of 1953 concluded that "it seems unlikely that Kilimanjaro will erupt destructively in the foreseeable future".

Selected Features of Interest

Brief descriptions of several features of particular interest, which may be seen near the normal route from Marangu, are added.

1. Lava Flows Near Horombo Hut

Directly below Horombo Hut, the lavas show interesting flow structures. The lavas themselves are rhomb porphyries with phenocrysts of white feldspar in dark groundmass. The surface of the flows solidified on cooling while the interior remained molten. The flow progressed by breaking through the crust forming at the snout, and the flows are long and narrow in shape. Mobility was retained because of the insulation from the cooling air and the sealing-in of the volcanic gases by the solidified crust. With the cessation of supply at the upper end of the flow, the molten material inside continued to flow down the slope leaving tunnels with steep parallel walls. The "super heat" of the interior re-fused some of the material of the walls, which re-crystallised as a glassy rock.

2. Zebra Rock

About 11/2 km. above Horombo Hut, west of the path, there is a low cliff with prominent light and dark vertical bands known as Zebra rock. The rock itself is a lamprobolite limburgite, an ultrabasic lava containing phenocrysts of titaniferous augite, olivine, and lamprobolite in a glassy matrix with small crystals of augite and iron ore. Biotite and anorthoclase occur in minor amounts. The light and dark colouration is superficial and is probably caused by encrustations from water percolating from the surface. The cliff extends northwards, parallel to the path, to the East Lava Hill on The Saddle.

3. Dyke-Swarm on Mawenzi

Most of the dykes, particularly those of the dyke-swarm, strike easterly and consist of trachydolerite, which contains platy feldspar and phenocrysts of augite and olivine. This material is hard and more resistant to erosion than the lavabreccias, tuffs and agglomerates which constitute the host-rocks. Consequently the dykes are left as prominent pinnacles and walls forming dramatic scenery. The group of pinnacles at the head of the corrie behind Mawenzi Hut is a magnificent example of this.

The margins of some of the dykes are finer-grained than their interiors, and have formed by the chilling of he magma against the host-rock. In certain instances these are harder than the interior of the dyke and have proved more resistant to erosion.

Although the majority of dykes on Mawenzi are composed of tracydolerite and have easterly strike, there are some which consist of olivine dolerite and strike northerly. Variations in the strike direction suggest the concentric pattern of ring dykes.

4. Kibo Rhomb Porphyry Lavas

The name rhomb porphyry is descriptive of the porphyritic crystals of anorthoclase feldspar which have rhombic cross-sections. These lavas are first encountered in the vicinity of Horombo Hut, but from the western side of The Saddle to the summit are the dominant rock-type. Some of the crystals attain considerable size, and Leedal (1955) has described examples of over 50 mm in length. The crystals weather out of the lava and can frequently be picked up in the screes. One of the best localities lies approximately mid-way between Gillman's Point and Uhuru Peak, where large white crystals have weathered out of the dark scoriaceous lava.

5. The Inner Crater of Kibo

The Reusch Crater, with its spectacular central vent of the Ash Pit, is perhaps one of the most perfectly formed examples in the world. It is probable that the crater has collapsed, as indicted by a feature on its western side called the Terrace, and fumarolic activity is located around the base of the crater scarp and the Terrace, following the fractures. The Ash Pit cone probably stood higher than at present and may even have formed the apex of the Inner Crater cone, reaching above the highest parts of the caldera rim.

The temperatures recorded at the mouths of the fumaroles are at the boiling point of water. A thermograph, installed and serviced for a period of 77 days in 1953, indicated a range from 77°C to 104.5° C, with a daily variation of about four degrees.

Much of the sulphur forms a thin crust less than 30 cm in thickness in the fumarolic areas. Sulphur may extend for depths of a metre around the vents. In places the sulphur occurs in long circular crystals, resembling the monoclinic allotropic form, and is very pure. The deposits were surveyed, drilled and pitted in 1951-52 by Sampson, Guest and Leedal and estimated to contain between 6,000 and 7,000 tons of readily available sulphur - fortunately insufficient to attract exploitation.

The sulphurous gases attack the lavas in the vicinity of some of the fumaroles and produce light-coloured alumina-rich clays, containing alunite, kaolin, and bauxite. These light-coloured patches are frequently surrounded by zones of red and brown-stained material indicating oxidation of iron enrich-ments, possibly suggesting small-scale basic fronts formed by the driving out of the iron by the action of the gases.

References:

N J Guest ad N Sampson: *Sulphur on Kibo, Kilimanjaro* (Min. Res, Pamp Geol. Surv Tang., 65, 1952).

F Jaeger: *Forschungen in den Hochregion des Kilimandscharo* (Mitt Deutsch Schutgeb, 22. 1909, p.113 and p.161).

F Klute: *Ergebnisse der Forschungen am Kilimandscharo* (Berlin 1920).

G P Leedal: *Anorthoclase Feldspar Crystals from Kibo* (Rec. Geol. Surv. Tang. 2, 1955, p.45).

H Meyer: *Der Kilimandscharo* (Berlin 1900).

R Reusch: *The Menelik Legend* (Tang Notes and Records 2, 1936, p. 77).

J J Richard: *Volcanological Observations in East Africa* (Jour. E. Afr. Ug. Nat. Hist Soc 18, 1945, p.1)

D N Sampson: *Notes on the Flora of Kilimanjaro* (Tang Notes and Records 34, 1953, p.68).

P C Spink: *Weather and Volcanic Activity on Kilimanjaro* (Geog Jour. 103, 1944,p.226).

W H Wilcockson: *Preliminary Notes on the Geology of Kilimanjaro*. (Geol Mag 93, 1956, p. 218).

Eric Shipton

ACCESS TO KILIMANJARO AREA

Kilimanjaro

The Davanu Shuttle is by far the most popular transport between Nairobi, Arusha and Moshi. From Nairobi, it costs 1,200 KSh each way to Arusha, and leaves daily from outside the Norfolk and New Stanley hotels. Both at Nairobi and Arusha, it leaves 08.00 and 13.00. Contact in Nairobi is 222002 (tel) and 216475 (fax).

Officially, it is a requirement to climb Kilimanjaro through a licensed tour operator, who will look after all costs. A typical 5-6 day trip up the Marangu route usually costs in the range of US$ 400-600. It is also mandatory to have a guide, but there are no standardised guide fees. There is now a quota restricting the number of visitors per day up the Marangu route.

Park fees for non residents:

Adults US$ 25 per day.
Hut fees on the Marangu route (irrespective of using them or not) US$ 25 per night.
Camping other than at the huts on the Marangu route US$ 40 per night.
Rescue fee US$ 20 per person per trip.

Tanzanian citizen park fees (guides and porters) to be paid at local rates of 1,500 TSh per day and 2,000 TSh per night. Note that this fees are subject to change without notice. Please contact the Park Warden for the latest rates.

Visitors approaching from Loitokitok (Kenya), must have Tanzanian guides and must obtain permits from the Marangu gate.

The nearest town to Kilimanjaro is Moshi, in Tanzania. Moshi can be reached by rail or bus, but perhaps the most effective way is by air to Kilimanjaro airport, some 34 km west of Moshi on main road Arusha. This modern airport is served by daily flights from Dar es Salaam, as well as international flights from Europe. There is a daily train service to Moshi from Tanga on the Tanzania coast. In Moshi there are two or three hotels and provision shops. These shops however, should not be relied upon to stock sophisticated mountain food.

Marangu, on the southern slopes of Kilimanjaro, is the normal starting place to climb the mountain. It is situated 11 km north of Himo, which is a village 27 km east of Moshi on the road to the Kenya border. There are two hotels at Marangu:

The Kibo Hotel	**The Marangu Hotel**
P.O Bo 102	P.O Box 40
Marangu	Moshi
Kilimanjaro	Tanzania
Tanzania	

Both these hotels arrange safaris on the mountain and hire out four-wheel drive vehicles, although these are no longer necessary for the Marangu Route. The normal route climb takes five days. More exact details of itinerary and costs may be obtained on application to either of these hotels. Bookings at the hotels should be made well in advance during the season.

The northern (Kenya) side of the mountain is not so accessible, and since the action of the Tanzania Government in restricting climbs from the Kenya side, the mountain must now be approached from Moshi. However, for completeness, the following information is included.

There is no hotel or other accommodation in Loitokitok, and the shops there are mainly for the local Masaai and have little of use to climbers. There is an Outward Bound School at Loitokitok but climbers should not expect the School to provide accommodation or other facilities. There is a bus service between Loitokitok and Emali (on the Nairobi-Mombasa road), but generally speaking a private car is needed to reach Loitokitok. It can be reached from Nairobi via the pipe-line track from Sultan Hamud (16 km north of Emali), or via the road from Emali itself. There is also a mountain road to Loitokitok from Marangu. These roads may be impassable during the rains.

Permits

Kilimanjaro National Park was opened by President Nyerere in June, 1977, and is administered by the Warden. The park headquarters is situated at the Marangu Gate at the start of the Marangu Route. Permission to ascend any route on Kilimanjaro must be obtained from the Warden who can be contacted at:

> **Kilimanjaro National Park**
> **P.O. Box 96**
> **Marangu**
> **Tanzania**
> **Telephone: Marangu 50**

Hotel Safaris and Porters

The Kibo Hotel and Marangu Hotel arrange complete safaris up Kilimanjaro, providing guide, cook, porters, all food and utensils, lamps etc. and booking the huts. Parties should give as much notice as possible, as it is sometimes difficult to fit in hut bookings and obtain porters. Climbers should provide their own boots, warm clothing, hat, dark glasses, sleeping-bag, first-aid outfit and anti-sunburn cream; but some of these items can be hired from the hotels.

The Kibo and Marangu hotels are also prepared to organise porters and their food for parties wishing to do the rest themselves. For up-to-date costings the hotels should be contacted direct. It is possible to organise an ascent of the Marangu Route without recourse to the services of the hotels. Except for the busiest seasons guides and huts can be booked at the Marangu Gate without much delay. However, parties who wish to climb Kilimanjaro as pleasantly as possible would do well to employ their porters through the hotels. They will hardly be able to do so more cheaply themselves, and in addition they will probably have to spend an extra day at Marangu trying to recruit porters and buy their rations. It is often difficult to obtain porters, particularly in December and January; there are many hotel parties at this season, and the local inhabitants are more profitably and less energetically engaged in picking the coffee crop. The porters are of the local Wachagga tribe and they are a cheerful and helpful people. They greatly appreciate the customary small tip for good service given at the end of the safari.

Inexperienced parties are advised not to do the climb without a guide and in any event all groups entering the park are required to have one. They do not carry a load, but they are responsible for organising the porters.

They remain with the party all the way to Gillman's Point or Uhuru Peak, and they can be of great assistance to weaker members of the party. Some fatalities on Kibo might never have occurred if a guide had been taken. Porters are also essential, as few people will have the stamina to carry their loads to Kibo Hut. Remember also that firewood and water have to be carried from Horombo Hut.

Mountain Huts

The main huts on Kilimanjaro are centred along the Marangu Route. "Mountain villages" might be an appropriate description of the huts located at the Mandara and Horombo sites. Mandara Hut, Horombo Hut and Kibo Hut should be booked well in advance. Bookings can be made either through the hotels at the base of the Marangu Route or through the National Park directly.

The huts and surroundings are often reported as being in a filthy condition. Parties are asked to make every effort not to throw litter about the mountain in general, and in particular to deposit refuse in the pits provided near the huts and to leave the huts cleaner than they found them

Mandara Hut (2,700 m), is the normal first night's stopping place on the Tourist Route, situated at the top of the true forest and just below the giant heath belt. The original hut, built before the First World War, is a stone building, which is now closed to tourists. There now exists a large central wooden chalet, surrounded by many smaller "chalet" style huts. Approximately two hundred people can be accommodated at Mandara. There is no shortage of water or wood fuel. This complex was built by Norwegians as part of an aid programme.

Horombo Hut (3,720 m), on the moorlands south of Mawenzi, is the second night's halt. Water is available from a nearby stream, but wood fuel is becoming scarce in the vicinity of the hut. This hut area is designed in the same style as Mandara with a large central hut, surrounded by many smaller huts. Again, about two hundred people can be accommodated.

Kibo Hut (4,703 m), is situated on the scree below the steep slopes forming the eastern side of Kibo crater. The original hut, built in 1932, contains four bunks and a stove. There is now a large hut accommodating many people, built in the style of a dining room with attached dormitories There is no vegetation at this altitude, and any fuel needed must be carried up from Horombo Hut; parties occasionally find enough ice near Kibo Hut to satisfy their water requirements.

Mawenzi Hut (4,600 m), is situated behind a small outcrop at the foot of the West Corrie of Mawenzi. It is usually reached by following the normal route from Horombo Hut to the rain-gauge at about 4,360 m on the saddle, then bearing right. It is small though six people can squeeze in; there is no porter accommodation. There is no fuel, but water is usually available from a small stream coming out of the West Corrie.

Mawenzi Tarn Hut (4,300 m). In 1969 a Miniport was carried to Mawenzi Tarn. This has now been erected but lacks glass

in the windows, and there is a snow-grass floor only. There is
room for about five persons. There is no wood for fuel.

Mweka Huts (3,100 m), are situated in the zone approximately
half a km. above the forest edge on the Mweka Route. The
two huts, both Maxiports, were established in 1966. Neither hut
is fitted with floor, bunks, or with any interior furnishings, but
each will sleep eight comfortably on their floors, and at a pinch
will take 12-14.

In the huts there is a small amount of equipment
including a paraffin lamp, a stretcher, and a box of first aid supplies. Wood is plentiful close by, and water is available from a
stream in a nearby ditch.

Barafu Hut (4,600 m), is situated on the ridge west of the
Southeast Valley, and is the upper hut on the Mweka Route. It
is a Maxiport, and was built in 1968. As with the Mweka Hut
there are no bunks. There is no wood available and normally
no water; both must be carried from lower altitudes.

Barranco Hut (3,900 m). Also known as the Umbwe Hut, it is
situated on a bench on the west side of the barranco. It was
erected in 1966. It is about 1/2 km off the Umbwe Route on
the trail which crosses the barranco at this elevation. The hut
is a medium-sized uniport with a burnt out wood floor that
sleeps six. Water is available nearby and there is a limited
amount of wood in the vicinity.

Arrow Glacier Hut (4,800m) is located near the little Arrow
Glacier at the foot of Kibo's Western Breach. It is the hut most
parties will use before making their summit bid from the Umbwe,
Machame and Shira Routes. Water is nearby but there is no
firewood. The hut accommodates six persons. The floor has
been burnt out. Note: this hut was destroyed by rockfall and
has not been rebuilt. You have to camp or make a bivouac.

Machame Huts (3,000 m), are situated at the edge of the forest on the Machame Route. Both huts are very basic Uniports, without floors or furniture. Water and firewood are nearby.

Shira Hut (3,840 m), is located on the Shira Plateau and is used by both the Machame and Shira Routes. It is an unfurnished Uniport. Water and firewood are nearby.

FOREST AND MOORLAND ROUTES ON KILIMANJARO

Owing to slightly lower rainfall and the lack of bamboo, the forest belt of Kilimanjaro is generally not quite so difficult to penetrate as it is on most sides of Mount Kenya. Nevertheless few people will readily desert the recognised routes which provide access to the moorlands from all directions.

1. Marangu route

This is by far most popular route; and, since it is by this route that the hotel safaris climb the mountain, it may quite accurately be called the "Tourist Route".

The route begins at the National Park Marangu Gate 1,800 m. It is a three to four hour walk through the fascinating rain forest to the Mandara Hut at 2,700 m, close by the Maundi Crater. One can reach Mandara Hut by either of two routes, the Eastern path being a relatively open track, while the Western is a narrow path cut in the undergrowth of the forest.

On the second day the route climbs steeply through the giant heath forest, but soon emerges from this and veers left (NW) across the moorlands on the southern slopes of Mawenzi. Horombo Hut is about 14 km (five hours) from Mandara Hut.

On the third day parties normally walk the 13 km or so to Kibo Hut. The route goes straight up the valley behind Horombo Hut and onto the Saddle - the wide, barren and comparatively flat area between Kibo and Mawenzi averaging 4,200-4,350 m in altitude. After Zebra Rocks and at the beginning of the Saddle a rain-gauge is reached; here the track forks, the right branch going to Mawenzi Hut (three hours from Horombo Hut) and the left branch crossing the Saddle to its western side, where Kibo Hut is situated.

The normal procedure is to spend the first night in Mandara Hut, the second in Horombo Hut, and the third in Kibo Hut. Then on the fourth day parties climb Kibo and descend to Horombo Hut for the night, and on the fifth day, the descent to Marangu is made. To do the ascent any quicker is to invite mountain sickness due to insufficient acclimatisation. There is quite a lot to be said for spending an extra night at Horombo Hut on the way up, but this might not be possible owing to congestion of hut bookings. At any rate, if you are going to be sick, try not to be so before reaching Kibo Hut!

2. **Mweka route**

The Mweka Route (Ref. R. Poppleton and A. Cormack, KMC Ice-Cap No. 4, Dec 1966; D. King, Unpublished Report, 1968), was opened up in 1965 and provides a route to Uhuru Peak and the Southern Glaciers that is as short as the Umbwe Route, but is much easier. The route is not as scenic as the Umbwe but it is safer and less likely to have the harsh weather sometimes experienced on the Umbwe. The route eventually joins up with the Barafu Route at the Barafu Hut (see Other Walking Routes on Kibo).

Mweka is situated 13 km. due north of Moshi. Walking begins at Mweka but in dry weather a four-wheel drive vehicle can proceed for a distance of approximately 4 to 5 km. beyond Mweka up into the forest. For the first 3 km. or so an old washed-out logging track is followed through the forest. This gives way to a path that leads a further 3 km. through the tree-heath zone to the treeline at 2,925 m. It is ten minutes more to Mweka Huts situated in a clearing in the bush-heath zone.

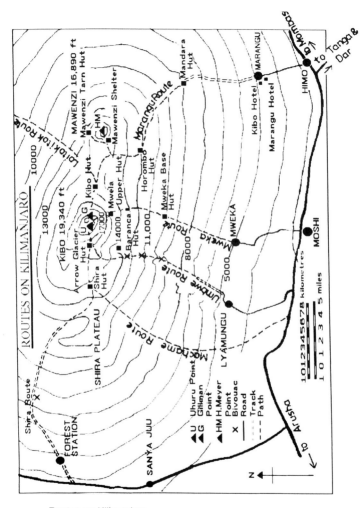

Routes on Kilimanjaro

The road from the Mweka Wildlife College to 2,000 m normally takes 2 1/2 - 3 hours to walk, and the trail from that point to the Mweka Huts a further 2 1/2 - 4 hours. Parties normally do not attempt to go farther than Mweka Hut on the first day as there is neither water nor shelter until much higher elevation are reached. The Mweka Huts, consisting of two unfurnished Uniports, can provide accommodation for twenty climbers. There is permanent spring water in a small valley below the huts to the south-east (5 minutes). Firewood is plentiful.

On the second day parties usually ascend to Barafu Hut. From Mweka Huts (don't forget your water!), the trail goes up a rocky rib through a zone of heath to 3,800 m (last wood). There it emerges onto open tussock grassland and at 4,100 m mounts the ridge east of the deep Msoo Valley. The ridge is followed up into the alpine desert to 4,500 m where it blends into the west ridge of the Southeast Valley. The trail then follows up the latter ridge to Barafu Hut at 4,650 m. This hut can accommodate 10 to 12 climbers. The Barafu Route is now followed to Uhuru Peak.

3. Umbwe Route

When opened up (ref. KMC Ice-Cap No. 2, June 1963), the Umbwe Route provided the shortest route to the Southern Glaciers and the Western Breach of Kibo. The more recently opened Mweka Route is probably shorter still (particularly to the Decken and Kersten Glaciers), and in addition, the new track to the Shira Plateau provides easier access to the Western Breach than does the Umbwe Route.

An ascent of Kibo by the Umbwe Route is one of the finest non-technical mountaineering expeditions in East Africa. It is a serious route, unsuitable for the solitary or the inexperienced.

From Moshi take the road passing Kindi Farm (bus route) for about 15 km. to the Mango-Kombo road. Turn right then left past Umbwe Mission and School, where cars can be left. The track is motorable for some distance. The footpath starts from the highest point of the track which is between two swampy dips. Though narrow it is not too badly overgrown though woodcutting obscures it in places. The path begins at 2,100 m and generally keeps to the narrow ridge crest between the Lonzo River on the west and the Umbwe on the east. After three to four hours (five to six from the forest boundary), Bivouac No. 1 (2,940 m), is reached, with a spring 15 m below under a rock face. It is an all-weather shelter, but there may be a lack of dry fuel if none has been left by previous parties.

Climbers who are really fit, not too heavily laden, and who have made an early start, may be able to push on the first day for a further four to five hours to Bivouac No. 2 (3,780 m) just under the first head-on view of the peak. There is as yet no shelter here except for an overhang. Water may be found 15 minutes down the ravine on the west; if this watercourse is dry, there is a permanent supply on the east side of the ridge, about 300 m lower. There is also a good cave at about 3,500 m with water only ten minutes away.

The tree line ends about 3,900 m. From here the path, which is cairned, to the Southern Glaciers branches right contouring into the Barranco. The Barranco Hut situated at 4,000 m is reached soon after starting the descent into the Barranco (2 hours from Bivouac No. 2). This hut, which is an unfurnished Uniport accommodates six persons. The path leads eastwards down the valley to a huge talus block at the point where all the glacier streams converge (good bivouac site). From here a scramble takes one up a vertical wall on the east (well cairned) to the moraine facing the Southern Glaciers. Access ways to these glaciers are now obvious, and the trail continues along he South Circuit Route. The route to the Western Breach from the tree line at 3,900 m continues up the Umbwe Ridge, which becomes the western lateral moraine of the Barranco. The moraine gives out onto the main slope of the peak and the route goes straight towards the Western Breach. The Arrow Glacier Hut is situated west of the little

Arrow Glacier at about 4,800 m. The hut has been destroyed by rockfall and has not been rebuilt. It is possible to camp or make a bivouac there. The route now follows the Western Breach Route to the summit (See section entitled Other Walking Routes on Kibo).

4. Machame Route

In the last few years the Kilimanjaro National Park Authorities have developed this route which lies between the Umbwe Route and the Shira Route. It joins the latter at Shira Hut (3,840 m). The Machame Route is a very fine way of ascending Kibo. The lower forest is very beautiful and the path is not quite as steep as the Umbwe Route.

The tarmac ends in the Machame village, and the four-wheel drive track to the left of the market place is followed over a bridge and for about 7 km. through the farms and forest to a curve where a sign post is seen on the right. Red paint marks the start of the forest path at about 1,920 m.

The route winds up through rain-forest and comes out in the heather at about 3,000 m (4 to 5 hours). The Machame Huts (2 Uniports) are located here. Water is plentiful in a stream five minutes down in the valley below the huts. From the huts cross the little valley and the route continues up the long steep ridge ahead. After some three to four hours the route veers west into a river gorge and from here continues westwards gradually ascending until the Shira Plateau is reached. Soon after joining the Plateau, one arrives at Shira Hut. Water is found to the north. From the hut the path to Arrow Glacier Hut is well signposted and cairned. It leads east from the hut and soon reaches the junction where the North Circuit Route leads of to the left. At this point the path continues eastwards crossing a wide valley then turning more south-eastwards towards the lava tower known as the Sharks Tooth. A little before the tower a route leads off rightwards to the Barranco Hut and the South Circuit Route. The left path leads to Arrow Glacier Hut and the Western Breach.

5. Shira Route from Kilimanjaro West

In 1968 the Kilimanjaro District Forestry Department constructed a track for four-wheel drive vehicles from West Kilimanjaro to the Shira Plateau. Until this track was built, access to the Shira Plateau had been by a poorly defined route up the north side of the Ngare Nairobi river (ref, this guide Book, 2nd Edition, 1963), or by route from Kibongoto (ref M Bigger, Ice-Cap No 4, Dec 1966). This track makes the Western Breach of Kibo very accessible.

The Shira Plateau itself possesses great beauty and an enchantment lacking on other areas of Kilimanjaro. Visitors must take note however, that altitude gain on the Shira Route can be very rapid, owing to the distance it is possible to cover in a vehicle. It is strongly recommended therefore that an extra day be spent at Shira Hut (3,840 m).

To reach the route drive out along the Moshi-Arusha road for 24 km, turning right at Boma la Ng'ombe and follow this road to West Kilimanjaro. At approximately 25 km gravel begins which is followed a further 20 km to where a forestry road (13 km) turns off right and leads to the National Park Gate at Londorossi Glades.

The track passes through 3 km of forest before coming to heath at 2,600 m. The next 8 km of track is up through heath, and though rough, is in good condition. This brings one to the edge of the Shira Plateau. In late 1968 the Mweka Wildlife College extended the track from this Point across the Plateau to the saddle between Shira Dome and the slope of Kibo at 3,740 m. The track passes through open heath, moorland, and rock, and crosses several streams. It was made with trucks and is just passable for its full length to four-wheel drive vehicles.

Approximately 3 km. onto the Plateau a road turns right to the Wildlife College camp on a fork of the Ngare Nairobi River. From the point where the road peters out, twenty to thirty minutes walk (well cairned) takes one to the Shira Hut (grid ref 083625). This hut can hold eight people. The hut is a suitable point for trips to Platz Cone and Shira Ridge.

From Shira Hut follow the Machame Route to Arrow Glacier Hut and/or Barranco Hut. The route is well cairned and signposted.

6. Northern routes from Loitokitok

The northern approach to Kibo is rather shorter than the Marangu Route. Unfortunately, access from Loitokitok is currently by the Tanzanian authorities. For further information, contact the Warden of Kilimanjaro National Park. The information following below is included in case the situation should change in future. Porters can be obtained through a local Sikh who can be contacted through the District Officer, P.O. Box Loitokitok - only one mail per week. The Outward Bound School runs a full series of courses and cannot be relied upon to organise parties, provides guides, or arrange Kibo Hut bookings. Cars should be left by arrangement with the D.O in Loitokitok.

There are several routes from the Loitokitok area, most of them opened up by Outward Bound, but they nearly all converge onto a single track below Second Cave (3,300 m), which is the usual first night's stopping place.

The old route from Rongai Forest Station (a few km. from Loitokitok and across the border in Tanzania) went past First Cave. The start of some other routes is rather confusing, as there has been a major afforestation scheme just across the Tanzania border. The "Naromoru" was, before access was restricted the only fixed route, and this is the route described here.

Coming from Rongai or Loitokitok, cross the Naromoru River and about 140 m after the bridge (and before the Forest Ranger's House and Forest Nursery) turn right up the mountain. Cars can continue up this track for a further 11/2 km. but it is not advisable to leave them here. From a point a few metres below the top of the motorable track the path leads off and crosses the Naromoru River to its true left bank. It con-

tinues through the forest with two or three other stream cross-
ings before the moorlands are reached.

Second Cave (five to six hours) can be seen on the
left of the moorland track on the other side of a stream, the
turn-off to the cave being just before a one metre rock step on
the main path. There are two other caves nearby, one 100 m
to the right above, the other a short distance beyond and to the
left of Second Cave, across another stream. If an Outward
Bound course is in occupation of one cave, the other may
have to be used. There is plenty of fuel around the caves -
and there is usually a stock-pile into the cave-mouths, which
should be replenished.

The Outward Bound School used to maintain a hut,
which is for the exclusive use of students taking part in O.B.
courses. However, in emergency it could be used as a shelter;
afterwards it should be left in a tidy condition. Such use and
the circumstances necessitating it should be reported to the
warden of the school as soon as possible.

The hut is situated at about 4,900 m behind a large
boulder, and is only seen from the lower north-east approach.
It is difficult to find. The hut is a large green metal hut, with a
wood floor but no facilities. It can accommodate a large party.

To reach Kibo Hut from Second Cave, continue up
the main path, crossing some stream beds; and after about
11/2 hours, Bread Rock (about 12 m high with small cairns)
comes into view. The path passes immediately to the right of it
and about 400 m further, on the far side of a wide stream bed,
is Third Cave (3,750 m). The Kibo path, which is cairned,
keeps straight on (do not take the right branch, which leads to
the Outward Bound hut). It aims for the lowest point on the
Saddle and continues to mount gradually until it meets the path
(which can be seen for some time), from Horombo Hut, just
below Kibo Hut. From Second Cave to Kibo Hut is about five
hours.

Third Cave is a possible intermediate campsite; it is
used by Outward Bound, but there are several other small

caves in the area. There is some fuel about, and water (if not available from the river-bed below the cave) may sometimes be obtained from a drip near the cave.

From Third Cave a path bears left to Mawenzi, and it is also possible to join the North circuit Route around Kibo.

7. Njara Route to Mawenzi

This route start from Njara School, 19 km. by road S.E. of Loitokitok (Marangu direction), just inside Tanzania. It is rarely used, but is the shortest approach to the Mawenzi barrancos and the northern part of Mawenzi.

From the school follow the motorable track a short distance to the Forest Ranger's hut on the edge of a steep valley. Go up the true right bank of this valley for about 11/2 km. until it can be easily crossed. Thereafter follow up the other bank until the confluence of the two barrancos is reached just below the forest. The gorges at this point are very steep, but it is possible to get down near the fire-break if access into the barrancos is required.

The route to the moorlands follows a game track which starts near the edge of the Little Barranco and follows up the true left side of the gorge into the forest. The path fades out higher up, but the route keeps close to the edge of the gorge all the way up. Just before the moorlands there is a steep rock face which may be turned on the right. The route now follows the ridge towards Wissman Peak.

Water is very scarce on this route, but may be obtained higher up by dropping into the valley on the west.

CLIMBING ON KILIMANJARO

There is no climbing on Shira, and the Kilimanjaro climbing routes are here divided into the Kibo section and the Mawenzi section. The first recorded traverse of the main peaks of Kilimanjaro was in September 1957 when A. Nelson, H. J. Cooke and D. N. Goodall went from Machame to Marangu tak-

ing in the ascents of Shira Peaks, Kibo and Mawenzi. In September 1971, P. Snyder and I. F. Howell traversed Kilimanjaro by ascending the Umbwe route, and ascended Kibo via the Western Breach Route. They then climbed Mawenzi, descended the East Face, and left the mountain by the way of the Downie Ridge.

With the recent reduction of glacial cover on all high mountain ranges of East Africa, there have been some considerable changes to the documented climbs. The MCK currently has no reliable reports of changes to the climbs on Kilimanjaro, but strongly advises climbers to proceed with caution.

For Climbing Standards attention is drawn to the section of this title in Part One of this book.

ROUTES ON KIBO (5,895 m)

Each year hundreds of people with little or no knowledge of climbing reach Gillman's Point (5,685 m), and many of them go 210 m higher to the highest point in Africa. This ascent can be made most of the year round, only the rainy seasons (mid-March to early June; and November to December), being inadvisable.

On the southern and south-western areas of Kibo, and some of the longest and most serious routes on the African continent have been established.

(1) Normal or Tourist Route
First ascent: The route taken by Lange and Weigele on 6th July, 1909, was virtually the same as this route.
Standard: A stiff walk. Care should nevertheless be exercised on the steep scree slope, as a slip may cause a dangerous fall, particularly on the descent.
Time: Four hours from Kibo Hut to Gillman's Point. A further 11/2 hours from Gillman's Point to Uhuru Peak, but may be much longer (or even impracticable) in bad snow conditions.

Kilimanjaro. The Marangu Route. Mawenzi viewed from the Saddle.

David Keith Jones

Parties usually leave Kibo Hut very early in the morning (by 3 a.m.) for the following reasons:

a) to get the benefit of frozen scree

b) to get a good view of the sun rising behind Mawenzi from high up

c) because it is quite a good thing not to be able to see the stretch of scree ahead of one; and

d) because one probably cannot sleep in any case.

Follow the well-defined track up the valley behind the hut, soon branching right into a subsidiary valley. At the head of this valley (about one and 3/4 hours from the hut) is a large overhang known a Hans Meyer Cave. Above this the route goes straight up very steep scree to reach the crater rim at Johannes Notch. Gillman's Point go either to the right or to the left of Bismarck Towers and continue clockwise round the crater rim, crossing one or two bits of glacier on the way. The slight eminencies of Hans Meyer and Elveda Points are passed before reaching Uhuru Peak, which can be distinguished by an oblong box containing the Kilimanjaro Mountain Club summit register book, and the brass plaque of the Tanzanian Independence Freedom Memorial.

Variation:

Instead of branching right soon after leaving Kibo Hut, continue in the same direction. The route veers right after an hour and follows a ridge below (and later almost beside), the Ratzel Glacier to Gillman's Point. This variation is of slightly less gradient and, holding its snow longer, can offer better condition that the main route. It is slightly longer in distance but not necessarily in time.

SOUTHERN GLACIER ROUTES

(2) **Ratzel Glacier**

This glacier has been climbed from Kibo Hut , the crater rim being reached near Stella Point. It is quite and easy climb with crampons (not above Grade II). This glacier has shrunk considerably in recent years. More recently the glacier has been approached, by members of an Italian alpine club, at the lower third of the side facing Gillman's Point. A 30 m ice cliff at about 60 degrees was first climbed and the upper slopes of the glacier was reached. From there, after a steep walk, the rim was reached near Stella Point. The ice climb, which required modern gear, took about two hours.

(3) **Rebmann Glacier**

This glacier has been climbed without difficulty, but has recently been neglected.

The major Southern Glaciers - the Decken, Kersten and Heim, provide more formidable climbs, white greater objective dangers. Because they have received fewer ascents and the glaciers have retreated considerably in recent years, gradings are less reliable. They should be attempted only be experienced parties, and it should be remembered that owing to their remote location, rescue is a difficult undertaking.

(4) **Decken Glacier Right Side**

First ascent: M. Tudo, J. Montford, F. Schock and J. Kuhn, Aug. 1974.
Season: January to mid-March and June to October. The latter season is better.
Standard: IV inf.
Time: 2 days.

From the right side of the ice tongue climb to a big rock (300 m), about 30 m below the right end of some ice cliffs. Then traverse right below rocks onto another icefield leading upwards. The rocks at mid-height are passed on the right on steep ice. After three pitches the more gentle slopes are reached to the east of The Wedge.

The lower sections of this route are exposed to rock and ice fall in the afternoon.

Kilimanjaro. The Southern Glaciers. Showing approximate Starts of the Routes.

Iain Allan

(5) Decken Glacier Original Route

First ascent: E. Eisenmann and I. Schnackig, 12th Jan 1938.
(ref Zeit. des. D. Alpenvereins 70, 1939).
Season: January to mid-March and June to October. Probably
the best conditions would be found in July.
Standard: III. This was the grading of the irst party.
Time: 2 days.

The lower 760 m of this 1,400 m climb, was reported
as steep with slopes of 50-55⁰ (and often up to 65⁰). Higher up,
the gradient gradually decreases. Much of the climb, including
short pitches of rock, should be tackled with modern ice gear.
Several icefalls were encountered. The first was by-passed on
the left; then came a smooth icefield which provided some of
the steepest climbing on the route. The second icefall was by-
passed on the right. Then a rock buttress was followed to the
third icefall, about 550 m above the foot of the climb. From
here the party veered right towards the rocks bordering the
glacier (bivouac site). An ice ridge was next followed, and a
fourth icefall was climbed before the slope began to ease off.

It is quite possible that the above description has
changed during the years since the first ascent. The route
could well be a grade harder than what it is stated above.

(6) Kersten Glacier Right Side

First ascent: I. J. Allan and M. Savage, 28th and 29th July 1976
(ref The Alpine Journal, Vol 82, No 326, 1977)
Season: January to mid-March and June to October.
Conditions on the first ascent were described as perfect.
Standard: V.
Time: 2 days.

The right side the Kersten is bordered by a prominent
rock buttress. Left of this the glacier is a confusion of overhanging seracs, with an icefield beneath them. Start beneath
the rock buttress and gain the icefield by a long traverse in
from the right. Up the icefield to its top left corner where a
gully rises up the left side of the seracs. Climb gully the tra-

verse rightwards through the seracs to a break leading up to easier ground, and a crevasse barrier, (5,100 m bivouac site). Straight up Southern Icefield to where ice steepens a little just below Uhuru Peak.

This long route (over 50 pitches), was described as very fine, but serious owing to afternoon icefall.

(7) **Kersten Glacier Direct Rroute**

First ascent: I. F. Howell, W. O'Connor and J. Cleare, 20th and 21st December, 1975.
Season: January to mid-March and June to October. Cloudy conditions were encountered on the first ascent.
Standard: VI.
Time: 2 days.

Start about the middle of the base of the Kersten and take the right hand couloir. Up the snow cone to the foot of the rocks where the couloir narrows and steepens. Climb a short ice step on the left to a snow ledge. Up the short rock wall to another snow terrace. Traverse right into a gully, and ascend steep ice (aid), and traverse right, back into the main bed of the gully. Climb to the rock overhang then move out left and up steepening snow to a small rock outcrop Straight up for several rope-lengths to a huge ice cliff. Four pitches up this onto steep snow leading to an enormous ice cave on the left (bivouac site). Move right and climb snow slopes to the Silver Saddle. Now follow the Original Route to the summit.
Variation: In January 1976, P Fatti and J Moss did a second ascent of the Direct Route, probably with variations just left of the line describe.

(8) **Kersten Glacier Original Route**

First ascent: W. Welsch and L. Herncarek, 20th, 21st and 22nd Sept. 1962 (ref M.C.K. Bulletin 55, 1962).
Season: January to mid-March and June to October.
Standard: VI
Time: 2 days.

Start at the left end of the glacier, and climb to a point below the first icefall (overhanging and about 30 m high). To avoid it a very hard traverse left was done to a steep icefield (4,955 m), from where there is an easier traverse right above the icefall. The second icefall (also overhanging), was avoided by moving over steep icefields and, finally, the Silver Saddle at 5,200 m is climbed. The final snowfields lead to Uhuru Peak.

(9) **Heim Glacier Direct Route**
First ascent: R. Barton and D. Morris, 29th and 30th Dec. 1977 (ref. M.C.K. Bulletin 75, 1978).
Standard: VI.
Time: 2 days.

Start just left of the steep rock barrier separating the Heim and Kersten Glaciers, and climb steep snowfields and short rock barriers to the base of the broad rock barrier below the upper seracs of the Heim Glacier. This is climbed by the right-hand gully, which on the first ascent was a steep twin icicle, giving a difficult 30 m pitch. Above, a short gully on the left was climbed, and then snowfields, first right then left, lead through a weakness between the seracs of the Heim and Kersten Glaciers. The upper snowfields are then followed to Uhuru Peak.

(10) **Heim Glacier Original Route**
First ascent: A. Nelson, H. J. Cooke and D. N. Goodall, 20th-25th Sept., 1957 (ref M.C.K. Bulletin 43, Dec, 1957).
Season: January to mid-March and June to October.
Standard: IV. Technically there is nothing harder than III sup.
Time: 2 days.

The route has been climbed in a day This is one of the classic ice routes in East Africa. It has received many ascents and is frequently done solo.

Start the climb above and to the left of the glacier snout. Ascend the tongue and surmount occasional small ice steps. After about 150 m move towards the left side of the

Kilimanjaro. Climbing on the Heim Glacier. *Ian Howell*

glacier (facing the mountain), and ascend an obvious gully which ends at the base of the steepest section of the glacier by a rock band. The steep section above is approximately 80 m in height. From this point either move up slightly rightwards then work back left to the end of the difficulties; or (probably easier), traverse 50 m leftwards along an obvious traverse-line beneath the rock band, then back rightwards along the top of the rock band following prominent lines of weakness. A short traverse left then leads to the top of the difficulties. At this point there is an excellent bivouac site located amongst the rocks which form the top of the Window Buttress. The route now ascends the easier angled snow slopes up rightwards, overcoming a small ice step (III) and leading to an obvious rock outcrop (bivouac site). From this point ascend the Southern Icefield up slightly leftwards towards the crater rim. Keep to the left of prominent ice cliffs, then bear rightwards to Uhuru Peak.

THE BREACH WALL

This massive 1,400 m wall is arguably the most serious mountain area on the African continent. Its great length, combined with altitude, avalanche danger, and dubious rock quality make it a very demanding undertaking.

(11) Breach Wall East End
First ascent: D. J. Temple and A. Charlton, 22nd and 23rd Dec. 1974.
Season: December to mid-March and June to October.
Standard: V sup.
Time: 2 days.

There is a stonefall danger on the lower section quite early in the day. From Arrow Glacier Hut make a descending traverse to the base of the wall to where an embayment is occupied by an ice slope. From this a hard rock pitch leads to a large icefield in the lower cliffs. Up this moving right across the foot of a great icefall to an icy groove. It leads to a ledge which is followed to the right over a rib and onto the lower part of the *Baletto Icefield*. Many rope-lengths up this to the foot of the upper tier (bivouac site). Traverse right to the edge of the Heim Glacier and up until there is a choice of continuing on ice or scree to the summit.

(12) **Breach Wall Direct Route**
First ascent: R. Messner and K. Renzler, 31st Jan 1978.
Season: December to mid-March and June to October.
Standard: VI.
Time: On the first ascent the entire route was climbed in a startling 12 hours. Future parties should allow at least 2 days.

From the Diamond Glacier a huge icicle hangs down the upper tier and its line is continued to the foot of the wall by an ice couloir. A direct route was taken to the start of the 80 m icicle. The icicle was then climbed and the route continued rightwards up the Diamond Glacier.

It is possible that the start of this route is shared with the Breach Wall East End Route.

(13) **Breach Wall Balletto Icefield**
First ascent: D. Cheesmond and D. J. Temple, 1st-4th April 1975.
Season: Probably most of the year.
Standard: VI.
Time: Allow 3 days.

Start left of the Breach Wall Direct Route and avoid the ice couloir and its overhanging base by climbing to the left. Six pitches of IV to V over steep variable rock requiring aid in places lead up and right to a point overlooking the couloir. A descending traverse on ice leads to the base of an icefall. Up this and exit right onto hard rock. Four rope-lengths up the ice to the base of the Icicle, which is the main problem of the Direct Route (good bivouac behind it). Now embark upon a long traverse to the right along the base of the upper tier to where it is broken by a gully (bivouac site at the base of a chimney to the left). Three hard pitches on poor rock followed by a traverse into the gully where the first ice pitch required aid.

Two more pitches lead to easy ground in the amphitheatre.

(14) **Breach Wall: Lortscher Route**
First ascent: F. Lortscher (solo), 11th and 12th Jan 1972.
Season: January to mid-March and June to October
Standard: V
Time: 2 days.

      Cross the Big Breach Glacier to the foot of the wall and climb a series of walls and ledges to the foot of the steep section. Up over weathered red rock to the western side of the Diamond Glacier and on to the summit.

(15) **Breach Glaciers Route**
First ascent: F. Lortscher and J. Mayer, 10th Jan 1972.
Season: Probably most of the year but would be more pleasant with plenty of snow on the upper screes.
Standard: III.
Time: One day.

      Start between the Breach Glaciers and pass behind the steep rock ridge at the head of the Big Breach Glacier. Up the scree and rock steps to Breschen Peak.

(16) **The Bastion**
First ascent: F. Lortscher (solo), 14th Jan 1972
Season: January to mid-March and June to October.
Standard: III
Time: One day.

      The route follows the easiest line up the rather broken rocks and snowfields of the central part of the Bastion - the mass of rock between the Breach and the Little Penck Glacier.

NORTH-WESTERN GLACIER ROUTES

(17) **Little Penck Glacier**

All except the top of this glacier was climbed on June 20th, 1969, by D. Payne and D. King. From a camp at the foot of the Great Penck Glacier, the party ascended the cliffs south of the Great Penck to the nose of the Little Penck. This proved difficult owing to bad rock and considerable melt ice, and it involved serious climbing and cutting steps up a deep trough. The lower part of the glacier, though steep (50-60 degrees) was easy because of good snow cover. Higher up the equally steep surfaces were of very hard melt ice. The party turned back just below the top of the rock cleaver (named Ravenstein by the Germans in the early 1900's) separating the Little Penck from the Great Penck (5,400 m). Since then the Little Penck in its entirety has been ascend, the remainder of the climb to the crater rim being relatively straightforward. The standard was about Grade III, and one day should be allowed.

A narrow ice tongue projects far lower than the rest of the glacier from its southern side, and this gives a good steep ice climb about Grade III.

(18) **Great Penck Glacier**
First ascent: J. Pike an P. A. Campbell, 14th Sept. 1960.
Season: Probably most of the year.
Time: One day.

The upper icefield can easily be reached by gullies in what once was the glacier's bed.

(19) **Pengalski Glacier**

Located on the south side of the Oehler Ridge, this is now the lowest body of ice on this side of Kibo It is an easy climb.

(20) **Drygalski Glacier**

The upper part of this glacier was apparently climbed

by E. Oehler and F. Klute in 1912. The easiest approach is from the south via the gap high in the Oehler Ridge. It is much reduced and is hardly more than a steep walk.

(21) Credner Glacier

This relatively easy climb has been done several times and it may be reached from the Loitokitok Route.

(22) North Glacier

This was climbed by H. Tichy in 1957, and is briefly reported in "Sui Ghiacciai Dell' Africa" by Mario Fantin.

On 31st December 1970 it was climbed by Fritz Lortscher alone. An unreported notch near the east end of the glacier was noted (it appears that the ice has receded some 300 m since 1930). The climb from the east end over the top of the glacier and down to the northern slopes of Kibo took 13 hours. The ice was very fissured with 18-20 steps, 3-12 m high on the way to the top. During the descent there were 16 abseils using ice belays. The return to the Saddle took the best part of a day over the waterless slopes of northern Kibo.

The Northern Glacier offers some superb ice scenery especially during the dry season when the ice is bare of snow. Visitors to the Reusch Crater may return to Gillman's Point along the side of the Glacier.

OTHER WALKING ROUTES ON KIBO

1. The Barafu route

This route begins from the Barafu Hut (approximately 4,500 m). Barafu Hut can be reached by way of the Mweka Route or the Marangu Route/Kibo South Circuit. This route is believed to have been ascended when the Kibosho Trail, 1 km to the west of the Mweka Trail was in use (1900's-1940's). The first modern ascent using the Mweka Route, to join the Barafu Route, was by A. Cormack in October 1965. This has since been repeated many times. The climb is only a stiff walk, except after heavy snow when it may become impassable without spending great effort an with possible step cutting. Six hours should be allowed form Barafu Hut to the crater rim, with a further hour to Uhuru Peak. The route is fairly well marked at the lower levels, but not so clear at higher altitudes. On the return journey timings can be reduced by more than half. The route is he most direct non-technical way to the summit, and therefore very steep, but it does not require specialised gear or climbing skills.

From the Barafu Hut continue up the ridge west of the South East Valley; at about 4,900 m the ridge blends onto the side of Kibo and a course is then set for the nose of the Rebmann Glacier.

One cliff-band is encountered which can be by-passed either on the left above high cliffs or on the right. At Rebmann Glacier (4,870 m), a slight jog north takes the route into the gap between it an Ratzel Glacier. This gap is followed up to the crater rim just west of Stella Point, where the Tourist Route is joined.

During the dry season of December to March all of the route is normally without snow but in the remainder of the year snow can be expected as low as 4,600 m. When it is bare most scree can be avoided as rock slabs are numerous. In descent from the rim to Barafu Hut great care must be taken to avoid getting into the South East Valley. Going into the valley is easily done even in good weather and once in it, it is rather difficult to climb out.

2. **The Western Breach Route**

This route begins from the Arrow Glacier Hut (approximately 4,800 m). This hut can be reached from either the Umbwe, Machame, or Shira Routes This way to the summit of Kibo via the Great Western Notch on the Crater rim does not involve any climbing above grade I scrambling, but an ice-axe may be useful on the snowfield. A compass should be taken, particularly for the descent, as cloud usually fills the

Breach later in the day. The Breach was descended by E. Oehler and F. Klute in August 1912. The date of the first ascent is not known; but members of the Sheffield University party ascended it in Aug-Sept 1953.

From the Arrow Glacier Hut, the way is fairly obvious, following a lava outcrop which forms a natural staircase through a spot in the cliffs, which are otherwise rotten. (The atrocious scree can be by-passed if crampons are used to climb the glacier).

After further scrambling on rock and scree (care is require not to lose the way here on the descent), one comes out onto the floor of the crater just north of the Furtwangler Glacier, at the western foot of the central ash-cone. Either skirt round the edge of the Furtwangler, or cross its western side where it falls over the cliffs (using crampons or an ice-axe for a short distance). Ascend the cirque or snow-gully between Furtwangler point and Uhuru Peak as snow conditions allow. Allow at least four hours for the ascent from Arrow Glacier Hut to Uhuru Peak. On the descent follow exactly the same route.

3. Route to the Inner Crater

The Inner Crater, also known as the Reusch Crater, lies in the northern part of the main crater of Kibo. To combine a visit to it with the ascent of Uhuru Peak makes a very long and exhausting trip Parties occasionally, however, make an ascent of Uhuru Peak, then bivouac inside the rim, in order to explore the Reusch Crater the following day; other sometimes make a visit to the Reusch in preference to reaching the highest point in Africa. They are rarely disappointed.

From Johannes Notch (Normal Route), instead of veering left to Gillman's Point, traverse north along the crater rim for 90 m, pass a bivouac site and descend down the screes below Leopard Point into the crater. Pass between ice-cliffs and walk WNW up the gentle slopes of the Reusch Crater to a point in the SE rim of the crater near a cairn (1 1/2 hours from Johannes Notch in good conditions).

From here the descent to the floor of the Reusch Crater is easy, and it is possible to view the fumaroles (usually active in the afternoon) and the sulphur deposits, or to reach the edge of the Ash Pit.

If time or snow conditions do not permit a descent into the crater, a good view of the Ash Pit and the Terrace may be obtained from a point on the rim of the Reusch Crater due south of the Ash Pit.

The Ash Pit (130 m deep), was descended in 1953 by C. Downy and P. Wilkinson, and again in 1954 by A. H. Firmin and D. N. Sampson. The screes on the eastern side of the Ash Pit were descended for 75 m to just above an obvious pinnacle. The ash and scree-covered slope to the right was then traversed for about 90 m to the top of a loose gully which leads down to the sloping floor on the northern side.

4. Walk round Kibo

First ascent: E. Oehler and F. Klute, 19th-28th September 1912. (ref E. Oehler 1915. "Von einer Forschungsreise am Kilimanjaro, 1912" Z.D.O.A. 46 pp 124-156).
Second ascent: P. Wood, D. King, M. Taylor and M. Blandy, 3rd-7th April 1969 (KMC party).
Standard: A stiff walk.
Time: Oehler and Klute took 10 days, but were carrying out a photogrammetric survey on the way. The second circuit was made in 3 1/2 days. Both parties begin and ended their circuits at Shira Plateau. Now with the development of the South Circuit Route, which connects the Horombo Hut on the Marangu Route, with the Barranco Hut on the Umbwe Route, a time of 3 days for the circuit would be reasonable for the average party.

A walk round the main peaks of Mount Kenya has long been a popular outing, but for unknown reasons a circuit of Kibo has never developed, although the scenery is superb and of great variety. The walk round Kibo is more of a small expedition than a walk. It cannot be done in less than three days after reaching elevations above 4,900 m and parties may wish to take longer. Tents should be taken for there are no huts non the north and west sides. The greatest problem is water, or rather, lack of water, and enough should be carried for at least one day, depending on where the party begins. Porters may not be available for the entire circuit, so parties should be strong experienced and self-reliant. The most likely starting place will be Horombo Hut on the Marangu Route.

From Horombo Hut (3,720 m), follow the South Circuit Route which is well cairned, beneath the icefalls of the Decken, Kersten and Heim Glaciers - this is perhaps the most spectacular trek on Kilimanjaro. The night is spent at the Barranco Hut (Barafu Hut being passed during the day), which is an altitude of approximately 3,900 m. This is a long day. From the Barranco Hut the track is followed for the Machame Route, before branching off north-eastwards towards the Lent Group. The track continues round Kibo at altitudes of 4,600 m and 5,200 m and the Northeast and north slopes are tiring and slow, as there are many small gullies and lava ridges and large areas of broken rubble. The track is followed round to the Saddle, and then the Normal Route is descended to Horombo Hut. Allow three days.

ROUTES ON MAWENZI (5,149 m)

There is no walking route up Mawenzi. All routes involve rock climbing and usually, in addition, some snow and ice work. Mawenzi rock has a bad reputation which is only partly justified, but care is always needed. It is hard climbing from any side and there is no route to the top for an ordinary tourist as there is on Kibo. However, Mawenzi Tarn is easily accessible from the north and spectacular views down the Great and Lesser Barrancos can be obtained by climbing the scree behind the tarn. Guides may not be available on this side of the mountain.

Description of routes on Mawenzi is made difficult because the nomenclature of peaks was for long uncertain, and many of the older accounts are either ambiguous or difficult to follow (e.g. Ice-Cap No. 1) or hard of access (e.g. some of the early German climbs).

(1) **Oehler Gully Original Route**

First ascent: E. Oehler and F. Klute, on 29th July, 1912 (ref. Zeit. des D. & O. Alpenvereins 1915).
Season: Most of the year.
Standard: IV inf.
Time: Half a day to the summit.

From Mawenzi Hut traverse left (north) along the scree past NW Corrie to the West Buttress. Climb up to the col on the NW Ridge above the buttress. Follow a line of beacons which lead upwards and to the right to the bottom of the *Big Step*. Traverse right along the base of this cliff to a narrow rounded gully which opens out above into a wide couloir *(Oehler Gully)*. In the gully for most of the year there are two icefalls. The lower one, in the narrow rounded portion of the gully, may present some problems, especially after a heavy rainy season.

The upper icefall, about 60 m higher up, should be taken on the right initially, followed by a traverse left above the icefall. It may also be completely by-passed by climbing out of Oehler Gully lower down and entering another gully further to the right. Oehler Gully leads up to a notch on the main ridge. Nordecke is to the left, and Hans Meyer Peak to the right, both may be reached in a few minutes. If descent is made by the same route, falling rocks may make the lower part of Oehler Gully unpleasant after mid-day, and detours out of the gully to the south may be necessary on bad rock.

In June 1969 a memorial plaque in memory of J. Hutchinson and F. Stevenson was placed at the start of the climb that led to their deaths on December 18th, 1967. This is at the bottom of the route, and the plaque is about 20 m above and the right of the start but easily seen.

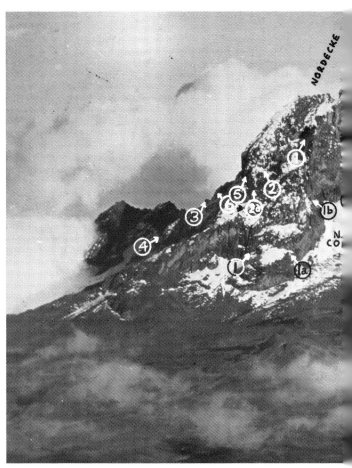

Kilimanjaro. Mawenzi. Showing Starts of Routes.

PURTSCHELLER
BORCHERS
KLUTE
LATHAM
PINNACLES
SOUTH PEAK
LONDT'S RIDGE
W. CORRIE
S.W. CORRIE

David Keith Jones

(1a) Oehler Buttress Variation

First ascent: W. C. West, O. Lennox-Browne and Miss S. G. Macdonald, 28th July, 1927 (ref. MCSA Journal 1927).
Standard: Not normally above III. If iced, the traverse into Oehler Gully may be IV.
Time: Half a day to the summit.

This route is often used in preference to the *Original Route*. Instead of traversing as far as the West Buttress, start the climb from the foot of the Oehler Buttresss on the north side of the NW Corrie. A series of easy chimneys leads to the scree platform on the buttress wall. Take either, and above the wall move generally left and climb down into a gully. Follow this gully upwards and it will eventually lead left into *Oehler Gully*. From here follow the *Original Route*.

(1b) North-West Corrie Variation

First ascent: R. A. Caukwell, P. A. Campbell, D. Bell, G. Low and L. Benito, 25th Dec. 1951. (ref M.C.K. Bulletins 22, Mar. 1952; and 27, Sept. 1953).
Standard: II (under ice-free conditions).
Time: Half a day to the summit.

Cross the NW Corrie to the middle of the face formed by the ridge bounding it on the north. The route on the first ascent started up the left-hand of two gulled at the top left-hand corner of the scree, and led, after about 60 m of scrambling and climbing on bad rock, to a ridge where it abuts onto a large buttress on the right. Any convenient route may in fact be taken up the middle of the face, traversing left when in doubt. Once the crest of the ridge is reached, a short scramble leads to a small gully (sometimes verglassed), which leads into Oehler Gully about 60 m below the upper icefall. The Original Route may now be followed.

(2) North-West Ridge Route

First ascent: R. F. Davies (solo), Jan 1953 (ref. MCSA Journal

1954, and M.C.K. Bulletin 33, March 1955).

Standard: II.

Time: Half a day to the summit.

Follow the *Original Route* (1), and traverse below the *Big Step* until about 25 m before the bottom of *Oehler Gully*. From here a narrow gully, on the right of a dyke, leads up the face and provides an easy route to the N W Ridge. The gully is best entered some 15 m up by an easy face on the right. From the top of the gully the ridge is followed to the summit of Nordecke, and then cross right to Hans Meyer Peak.

(2a) North-West Ridge Direct Variation

First ascent: R. F. Davies and J. V. de Graaff, 4th Feb. 1954 (ref. as for North-west Ridge Route).

Standard: III.

Time: Half a day to the summit

Instead of climbing the gully described under (2), climb the Bigstep directly - about 60 m of Grade II and continue up the North-West Ridge

(3) North Spur

First ascent: D. Knowles and J. Kempson, 5th Sept. 1972.

Standard: V.

Time: 8 hours.

From the scree next to the spur traverse right onto the ridge. Follow this to where a long diagonal gully meets the ridge. Climb the red wall on the other side of the gully starting on the left of an orange dyke, regaining the ridge in two pitches. Go up a ramp below a huge white wall to a col. Continue up a purple band and traverse left to a window. A broad chimney leads to the North-west Ridge which is followed to summit of Nordecke. Hans Meyer Peak is reached over to the right.

(4) North-East Ridge

First ascent: R. F. Davies and J. V. de Graff, 5th Feb. 1954 (ref. MCSA Journal 1954 (with photo), and M.C.K. Bulletin 44, March 1955).

SKETCH MAP
OF
MAWENZI

SCALE IN METRES

KEY:

➤➤➤   Ridge

⌢ ⋯   Top of scree

⊨   Col

△   Peak

H.M.P. = Hans Meyer Peak
P.P. = Purtscheller Peak
B.P. = Borchers Peak
K.P. = Klute Peak
L.P. = Latham Peak
S.P. = South Peak
N. = Nordecke
W.P. = Wissman Peak
② ➤ START OF CLIMBING ROUTE

Sketch Map of Mawenzi.

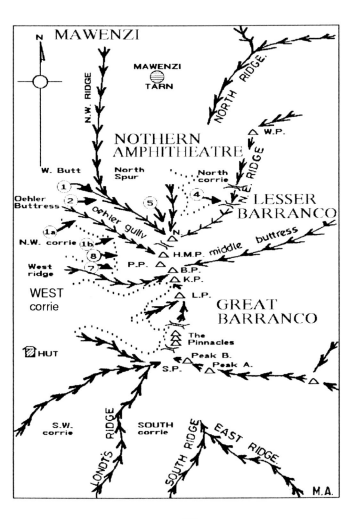

Standard: III, with one pitch of IV in January or February.

From Mawenzi Hut go north, cross the NW Ridge low down, thence across the Northern Amphitheatre past the North Spur towards the NE Ridge. From the scree slope enclosed by the North Spur and the NE Ridge a prominent ledge runs diagonally left up to the higher of two notches on the NE Ridge. The climb starts at the bottom of this ledge and goes up to the Notch. On the first ascent four hours were taken to reach the Notch. Steps had to be cut, and a large ice-covered chockstone just below the Notch was avoided by climbing out left on unsound rock (IV). In October this ledge has been found ice-free, but with much loose rock, and the chockstone was climbed direct. The steep face on the ridge above and to the right of the Notch provides 18 m of climbing. After a traverse right for about 12 m the route again goes up to the ridge, generally keeping little to the right of the crest and following a discontinuous black dyke on sound rock. This leads to the north end (Nordecke) of the main ridge, and Hans Meyer Peak may be reached by crossing the gap at the top of Oehler Gully.

(5) **North Face Direct**
First ascent: M. Tremonti with guide M. Bianchi, 4th Sept. 1958 (ref. Journal of Friulana section, C A I :"In Alto" 51, 1957-58).
Standard: V.
Time: Half a day to the summit.

Walk to the Northern Amphitheatre and go up the scree slope between the North Spur and the NW Ridge. From near the top of the scree along diagonal line goes straight up towards a large vertical *Triangular Face*, where the crux is. From the start the first 150 m of climbing (II) brings one to the base of a 90 m red cliff below the Triangular Face.

Climb the cliff for 40 m bearing slightly right (II), and then 60 m on a rising traverse to the right (III) as far as a couloir, which is climbed for about 60 m, up "loose earth and stones" to the bottom of the Triangular Face. A red crack runs about two-thirds of the way up this face, and it is climbed for 40 m on bad rock with considerable exposure (V). Move out to the left, and climb on sound violet-coloured rock to the summit of Nordecke, from which Hans Meyer Peak may be easily reached.

(6) **North Face Traverse**

First ascent: R. Smith, A. Jenkins, N. Harte and P. A. Campbell, 29th Dec. 1960 (ref. м.с.к. Bulletin 52, June 1961).
Standard: III. Beware of loose rock and stonefall later in the day.
Time: Half a day to the summit.

Follow the *Original Route* (1) to the base of the *Big Step* on the NW Ridge. Traverse round onto the North Face and continue on a rising traverse across many gullies and some bad rock ridges, generally keeping as high as possible, until the NE Ridge is reached just below Nordecke. The gully to the south of Nordecke leads to the head of Oehler Gully, from where the summit may be reached.

(7) **Outward Bound Route from the West**

First ascent: S. L. Summers, E. D. Stroud, and K. R. Nievens, Feb. 1957 (ref м.с.к. Bulletin 43, Dec. 1957).
Standard: IV.
Time: 10 hours.

From Mawenzi Hut traverse left (north) into the NW Corrie and walk up the scree to a gully in the top right-hand corner. This gully may have been the one descended in 1889 by Hans Meyer and Purtscheller after the first of their attempts on Mawenzi. Climb the gully, avoiding the first icefall but climbing the next two; then ascend a very steep slope topped by a vertical rock face, which may be by-passed on the right. At the head of the gully climb out on the left-hand wall on quite good rock onto a sharp arete. Turn right and climb this until a steep smooth slab prevents further progress. Climb across the top of the steep snowfield below Purtscheller Peak, then up a long snow-face to a gully leading to the main ridge. Climb up to the left of the gully on rock to the ridge, and then after a long final rock pitch bear right to the summit.

(8) Firmin Route from the West
First ascent: A. H. Firmin and D. N. Sampson, 1954.
Standard: IV.

The route started up a gully in the steep face between the West Ridge and *Oehler Gully.* Higher up a wall was climbed, and a difficult pitch led round a corner onto a prominent nose. The nose was followed until it petered out, then a diagonal traverse left led to the West Ridge of Hans Meyer Peak, which was followed to the summit.

This route seems to be much the same as the one followed by Tremonti on the SW Face of Chiglione Tower.

OTHER MAWENZI PEAKS
Wyss-Dunant and Chiglione Towers

These are on the West Ridge of Hans Meyer Peak. The higher Wyss-Dunant Tower is not very prominent, but the Chiglione Tower has rock faces falling into Oehler Gully and the NW Corrie.

(1) North Face of Chiglione Tower
First ascent: P. Chiglione and E. Wys-Dunant, 16th Jan. 1937. (ref. Wyss-Dunant: Mes Acensions en Afrique, Paris 1938). *Standard:* IV.

The vertical rocks of the North face were climbed from Oehler Gully.

(2) South-West Face of Chiglione Tower
First ascent: M. Tremonti with guide M. Bianchi, 8th Sept. 1958 (ref. CAI "In Alto" 51, 1957-58). *Standard:* V. *Time:* 3 hours.

The route starts from the highest point of the scree in the centre of the N W Corrie at the bottom of a steep couloir. A narrow chimney is climbed for about 15 m (V), followed by some 60 m of easier climbing up the couloir, with a danger of falling rock. Traverse up to the left onto the big face. After about 75 m there follows another 75 m of poor fluted rock to a wide ledge sloping up to the right This is followed round, then up a couloir to the notch between Chiglione and Wyss-Dunant Towers. From here there is an easy ridge followed by a little chimney to the top. The notch also provides easy access to the Oehler Gully for the descent.

Purtscheller Peak (5,120 m approx.)
This peak, the second highest on Mawenzi, was first climbed on 9th Jan. 1938 by E. Eisenmann and R. Hildebrand as part of their traverse of the Mawenzi Peaks (ref. Zeit. des D Alpenvereins 70, 1939). The climb appears to have been done from the snowfield on the western face. No standard is given.

Borchers Peak (5,115 approx.)
This peak, described by Eisenmann as the "twin" of Purtscheller Peak, used to be named "Un-named I". The first ascent, "without great difficulties", was also made by Eisenmann and Hildebrand on 9th Jan. 1938, the ridge being followed from Purtscheller Peak.

Klute Peak (5,095 m approx.)
This peak was apparently the peak climbed by H. Meyer and L. Purtscheller on 15th Oct. 1889, in their attempt to reach the main summit (ref. H. Meyer: First Ascent of Kilimanjaro, 1891). It was for a time called Purtscheller Peak, and then "Un-named II". The route is not known, but they may well have followed a fairly obvious line which goes up the northern branch of the West Corrie. At the head of this couloir which may be climbed to the ridge, from which the peak may be reached.

The peak was climbed as part of the great traverse by Eisenmann and Hildebrand, who made a "difficult" ascent from the NW. On the broad flat summit are some magnetic rocks.

Latham Peak (5,067 m approx.)
This peak was first climbed by D. V. Latham with the African guide Oforo on 7th July, 1926 (ref. Geog. Jour. 68, Dec. 1926). It may be climbed either from the north or south. From some angles (e.g. from near Mawenzi Hut) the southern shoulder looks like a separate peak, which is not.

The Pinnacles
These lie between Latham and South Peak, and they have been named from north to south: Cortina d'Ampezzo, Gorizia, Udine and Scoiattoli di Cortina (after sections of the CAI).
First ascent: M. Tremonti with guide M. Bianchi, 6th Sept. 1958 (ref. CAI "In Alto" 51, 1957-58).
Standard: V.
The traverse of these pinnacles starts high up the scree and to the north of Cortina d'Ampezzo. A gently rising traverse leads to a point on the west side below the col between the first two pinnacles. Climb up and to the left to reach the first peak from the NW, abseil onto the col and climb the second peak also from the NW. Climb down to the next col, by-pass a gendarme on the west, and climb the third pinnacle also on the NW side (IV). Abseil to the scree and climb the last pinnacle (which is too small to stand on) from the south over thin rock (V)

South or Londt Peak (4,985 m approx.)
This peak was first climbed from the west in December 1924, by G. Londt with the African guide Oforo and a porter (ref. MCSA Journal 1934).
It has been climbed by R. Hildebrand and K. von

Wuest in Jan. 1938 from the pinnacles; they descended by the SW Ridge and encountered some difficulties. M Tremonti in September 1958 also made the ascent from the Pinnacles, but he by-passed the difficult vertical sections of the north side by traversing round to the right almost to Londt's Ridge.

South Peak was climbed from the south on 10th Feb. 1961 by F. Lortscher with a local guide. They ascended across the western scree, passing big boulders, onto a rocky knoll, from which an easy traverse across sand and boulders below the rock was made in the direction of the notch between South Peak and Peak B (the higher one of peaks A and B). Ascent of the South Face was started after traversing about 200 m. The height of the face was about 320 m. The grading was II with a few pitches of III. A helmet was reommended owing to stonefall The time taken was 7 hours for the round journey from Mawenzi Hut (ref Letter MCK 21.4.61 and KMC 14.4.61).

Peaks A and B
These twin peaks, on the ridge east of South Peak, were climbed by N. R. Rice (solo) on 23rd Jan. 1932 (ref Ice Cap No. 1, 1932). Peak A (the eastern one) was easily climbed from the SE. Peak B was climbed by a couloir in the south-west corner, followed by a delicate balancing move on rotten rocks to reach the summit rocks, from where there is a fine view of the East Face of Mawenzi.

Raoul Peaks I, II and III
These three gendarmes on the South Ridge of Mawenzi were climbed by Rice on the same day that he climbed Peaks A and B. The total round trip from Horombo Hut took ten hours.

Wissman Peak (4,800 m)
This peak, on the NE Ridge of Nordecke, was apparently first climbed on 5th Feb, 1954, by I. Keith and Miss J.

Slinger (ref MCSA Journal 1954). The route started from the
Northern Amphitheatre and followed easy rock (not above III)
on the SE Face. More recently a new route has been put up:

(1) North-East Face of Wissman Peak

First ascent: K. F. Ledward and T. S. Robertson, Feb. 1963.
Standard: IV

From the col on the SW of Wissman Peak descend
about 100 m down the gully towards the Lesser Barranco as
far as the foot of a large flake. This flake is climbed 18 m to a
sentry box. Climb a thin crack to the right for 11 m. Traverse
right onto the wall, and thence up some 12 m to a piton stance
under the overhang. Traverse left about 3 m to the end of the
overhang. A short hand-traverse and a mantle-shelf lead to
easier, though poorer rock. Climb this for about 18 m and then
traverse left into the foot of a shallow chimney. This is climbed
on the right-hand side on poor rock.

TRAVERSE OF MAWENZI PEAKS

First ascent: E. Eisenmann and R. Hildebrand, 8th-10th Jan.
1938 (ref. Zeit. des D Alpenvereins 70, 1939).

The *Original Route* up Oehler Gully was climbed,
and the first night spent between Hans meyer and Purtscheller
Peaks. The next day they climbed a difficult wall onto a snowfield, up to a snow col, and then left up to Purtscheller summit.
The ridge was followed to Borchers Peak. They then descended slightly left, made two short abseils and traversed to the
right of the ridge going round a rock tower. Klute Peak was
climbed with some difficulty, and their second bivouac was
beyond this peak. On the third day they crossed easy ground
to Latham Peak.

Mawenzi has also been traversed from south to
north by Fritz Lortscher on 28th-30th July 1969. From
Horombo Hut, South Peak was climbed via the East Face (a
new route). The first bivouac was after Latham Peak. The fol-

lowing day Klute, Borchers and Purtsceller Peaks were climbed on route to the summit, Hans Meyer, which was reached in the late afternoon. The main difficulty was between Borchers and Purtscheller Peaks where the route followed narrow iced up gullies. Rock falls were encountered here as well as on the East Face of South Peak. After visiting North Peak the descent was made with a bivouac on the Saddle. The time for the round trip from Horombo Hut was 58 hours.

EAST FACE OF MAWENZI

The terrain here is very difficult and little explored (ref. MCK Bulletins 36, 38 and 39 of 1955 and 1956). If the weather is clear, fine views of the precipitous East Face and of the spectacular Great Barranco may be obtained by walking to the top of the scree of the West Corrie (behind Mawenzi Hut), where there are two cols between Latham and South Peaks - the one to the south of the Pinnacles being easier of access.

The two very deep gorges as the Great and Lesser Barrancos start on the eastern side of Mawenzi and run generally NE to meet just below the forest. They have been crossed once by A. H. Firmin and J. W. Howard with two bivouacs on the way. Access to the southern wall of the Great Barranco is from Horombo Hut or Mandara Hut. The northern side of the Lesser Barranco may be reached by traversing around from the Saddle below Wissman Peak, or via the Njara Route.

The East Face of Mawenzi is almost virgin climbing ground; and owing to its difficulty of access, it is not likely to become much frequented by climbers. In 1953 Downie, Firmin, and Wilkinson traversed onto the East Face from Three Kings Valley on the S. E. rim; they crossed the main gully which terminates near South Peak and climbed some distance up the face below Latham Peak (ref. article by W. H. Wilkinson in Geol. Mag. 93:3, 1956).

In 1964 two RAF climber, Fl. Lt. Edwards and P. T. I. Cpl. Thomson, climbed the East Face, up a 230 m ice couloir between Nordecke and Hans Meyer peaks, which involved pitons and serious climbing. This couloir has been descended during a traverse of Kilimanjaro by I. F. Howell and P. Snyder in Sept. 1971. On 5th-7th March 1970 Fritz Lortscher alone made what appears to be a similar approach: he passed a crashed Dakota, and traversed to the upper part of the Barranco, where he bivouacked without water. After 14 1/2 hours climbing next day he reached the crest of the ridge near Latham Peak, where he spent his second night. The route is described as grade II-IV, with two pitches in the upper part of V. From 11 am there were rockfalls all over the face and "one is lucky not to get hit". Other difficulties were cloud which obstructed route-finding, sharp rock which cut his hands, and untrustworthy rock. He found a little ice and snow in crevices.

Rock falls are probably less likely immediately after the rains when the face is iced up. This is the case on the western faces where iced up routes are generally chosen in preference to pure rock routes. Attempts to approach via the Barrancos from the bottom have failed, and do not seem practical. However the ridge between the two Barrancos which leads to the East Face has been climbed by I. F. Howell and R. F. Higgins in July 1968. The route graded III/IV and three bivouacs were needed before the summit was reached.

HISTORY OF CLIMBING ON KILIMANJARO
1862 - 1889

After John Rebmann, the CMS missionary, who first saw the snows of Kilimanjaro from the plains to the east, on 11th May, 1848, an interval of over 14 years elapsed before any attempt was made to set foot on the higher slopes of the mountain. In November 1862, the explorer Baron von Decken, accompanied by Otto Kersten, reached a height of about 4,300 m. It was another missionary, Charles New, of the Methodist Mission at Ribe, near Mombasa, who on 28th August, first reached snow on the saddle. Other visits were made by Dr.

Fischer (1883), H. H. Johnston (1884), Count Teleki and Von Hohnel (1887).

This exploratory period came to an end with the climbs of Professor Hans Meyer, the Leipzig geographer, with his guide, Ludwig Purtscheller of Salzburg, in 1889 - an interesting parallel to the climbs of the geography Professor Mackinder with his guides on Mount Kenya 10 years later. Hans Meyer had already reached 5,500 m on Kibo in 1887. Two years later he organised another expedition, and together with Purtscheller did the following climbs:

3rd Oct -   reached the crater rim via the Ratzel Glacier.
5th Oct -   made the first ascent of the highest point of Kibo, 5,895 m, via the Ratzel Glacier.
15th Oct - climbed Klute Peak on Mawenzi.
18th Oct - again reached the crater rim of Kibo at Hans Meyer Notch.

References:

C. New: Life, Wanderings and Labours in East Africa (1874). Also article in Alpine Journal (Vol.6, 1874, p.51).
H. H. Johnston: The Kilimanjaro Expedition (1886). Also article in Proc. R. Geog. Soc. (Vol. 7:3, 1885).
H. Meyer: Zum Schneedom des Kilimanjaro.(1888) Across East African Glaciers (London 1891). Kilimanjaro. Proc. R. Geog. Soc. (Vol. 12, 1890).

1890 - 1918

The Meyer-Purtscheller climbs were not immediately followed up, and it was in fact Meyer himself, this time with E. Platz, who next reached the crater rim in 1898. In October that year Captain Johannes Korner opened up a route from Moshi and reached the crater rim at Johannes Notch, also climbing the rocky eminence to the south of the notch (Gillman's point). Others to reach Johannes Notch in the early years of the 20th century were: Dr. Uhlig (who examined the glaciers), Paymaster Muhlhauser, Assesor Gunzert, Dr. F. Jaeger, W. Methner (District Officer, Moshi), Dr. E. Forster, Dr. Ahlbory and Herr Rohrbeck.

On 6th July, 1909, two surveyors, M. Lange with his assistant Weigele, made the second ascent to the highest point of Kibo (then called Kaiser Wilhelm Spitze) via Johannes Notch, i.e. by the line of the present Tourist route, and they went on from Kaiser Wilhelm Spitze to look down into the Great Western Breach from Furtwangler Point. Three years later important climbs were made on Kibo and Mawenzi by two parties. On 29th July, 1912, E. Oehler (who had been on Kibo with Jaeger in 1906) and F. Klute (glaciologist) made the first ascent of Hans Meyer Peak, the highest peak on Mawenzi.

They next made the first ascent to the Kibo crater from the west (via the upper Drygalski Glacier), descending by the Western Breach. A few months later a Munich climber, W. Furtwangler, with S. Konig made the third ascent of Kibo summit - on skis. The same pair also made the second ascent of Hans Meyer Peak on Mawenzi.

By this time ascents of the lower slopes of the mountain were becoming easier. The path from Marangu was now established, and Bismarck (Mandara) and Peters (Horombo) Huts had been built by Dr. E. Forster for the German Kilimanjaro Mountain Club. The outbreak of war in 1914 prevented the planned construction of a higher hut, where Kibo Hut now stands; and the Hans Meyer Caves lower than this site were used by all climbers for their final bivouac. The original cave was about ten minutes down the track from Kibo Hut, and was originally known as "Nyumba ya Mungu" or "House of God" by the Wachagga tribe. The cave now known as Hans Meyer Cave was lost in time and memories. War put a temporary stop to climbing, but not before two other ascents of Kibo had been made in 1914. Two artists, W. von Ruckteschell and C. von Salis made the climb, and Frau von Ruckteschell accompanied them as far as the crater rim (being the first woman to do so) A few months later W. C. West (MCSA) made the ascent.

References:

The Ice-Cap No 1 (1932) - Journal of Mt. Club of E. A.
F. Klute: Die Ergebnisse der Forschungen am Kilimanjaro (1920).
Various articles in Geog. Journal by Johannes (Vol 13, 1899), Uhlig (vol 25, 1905), Jaeger (Vol 29, 1907) and Klute (vol 40, 1912; Vols 60, 1922 and 61, 1923).

1919 TO DATE

After the war Kilimanjaro lay in British Trust Territory. In 1921 a large expedition was organised, and C. Gillman and P. Nason raised the Union Jack at Johannes Notch and climbed the rocky eminence which now bears Gillman's name. Their attempts to go further to the summit of Kibo were frustrated, as were the attempts of a similar flag-raising party 30 years later. Several ascents of Kibo were made between 1925 and 1927, by G. Londt of MSCA, three times by Rev R. Reusch, by W. West again with Miss S. McDonald - the first women to climb Kibo and also to make the ascent of Latham Peak (Mawenzi) and by C. Zeidler. Many of these parties were accompanied by one or other of two African guides - Johnathan and Oforo. Also in 1927 also started a period of scientific activity started on Kilimanjaro. Mosterz, a volcanologist, Nilsson, a Pleistocene geologist, Cotton, a botanist, Jaeger, a glaciologist, Moreau, a zoologist and Geilinger, a glaciologist, all visited the mountain. In 1930 the Swiss airman Mittlelholzer flew over Kibo and took photographs.

An important event of this period was the foundation at Moshi in July 1929 of the Mountain Club of East Africa, of which the Kilimanjaro Mountain Club is now the successor. The most prominent founder members were C. Gillman, N. R. Rice, P. Ungerer and Rev Dr. R. Reusch, who averaged three ascents a year, of the Lutheran Mission at Marangu. The long delayed Kibo Hut was built in 1932, and hotel safaris were organised with porters and guides, many of whom made the ascent over a hundred times. From this time on Kilimanjaro has become more and more popular, with large numbers of people reaching Gillman's Point each year, and rather more select band continuing to the highest point. The scope for climbers has also increased, with routes of considerable difficulty having been opened up via the Heim and Kersten Glaciers on Kibo Mawenzi Hut has made climbing easier on that mass. In 1938 Eisenmann's expedition did a traverse of the peaks of Mawenzi, and several new routes have since been pioneered up Hans Meyer Peak.

Since the Second World War there have been several interesting developments. Sheffield University sent an expedition in 1953 which made a full study of the geology of the mountain; and again in 1957 a Sheffield expedition, containing many of the members of the earlier expedition, studied the glaciology as part of the International Geophysical Year programme. An East African Outward Bound School was founded at Loitokitok, on the Kenya side, and the culminating feature of each course has been the ascent of Kibo. During the 1960's organised parties of boys from Nairobi schools made mass ascents to Gillman's Point. On 18th May, 1955, there was a disastrous air crash at 4,600 m on the SE slopes of Mawenzi, all the passengers and crew of E. A. Airways Dakota being killed.

Kibo has recently become the venue for various stunts, with parachutists landing in the crater, a party playing tidily winks on the summit and many other gimmicks. Records for the ascent of Kibo have been made by Outward Bound instructors and others, the present fastest time from Loitokitok to Uhuru Peak and back being 13 hours 20 minutes - done overnight.

When Tanganyika achieved self-government in December 1961, it was decided that the national flag should be raised on the highest point in Africa. Unfortunately it had to be raised at Gillman's Point due to exceptionally bad weather and snow conditions, making the traverse around the crater rim impossible. However, a year later on Republic Day, 9th December 1962, the flag was carried up and raised on the highest point of Kibo, now renamed Uhuru Peak.

The 1970s have seen several important developments, both in mountain administration and climbing achievements. In June 1977, President Nyerere officially opened the Kilimanjaro National Park, with headquarters at the Marangu gate. The Tourist Route from Marangu has seen considerable changes with the erection of sophisticated hut complexes, largely as a result of aid from Norwegian Government. There has recently been much climbing developments on the remote South-west side of Kibo with major routes being climbed on the magnificent Breach Wall. F. Lortscher and D. J. Temple being the prominent pioneers in this decade. The crowning achievement of that decade however, must surely to to R. Messner and K. Renzler for their fine ascent of the Breach Wall Direct Route in 1978.

References:

C. Gillman: An ascent of Kilimanjaro (Geog. Journal Vol 61, 1922).

D. V. Latham: Kilimanjaro (Geog. Journal Vol 68, 1926).

P. Gutmann: Article on Londt's climb (Alpine Journal Nov. 1926).

W. Geilinger: der Kilimanjaro, sein Land und seine Menschen (Bern 1930).

Tanganyika Notes and records, No 64, March 1965, articles on information of historical interest on Kilimanjaro.

I. J. Allan: The Alpine Journal, Vol 82, No 326, 1977.

PLACE-NAME ON KILIMANJARO

Rebmann in 1848 said that *Kilimanjaro* was a Swahili word meaning "Mountain of Greatness", but it could also mean "Mountain of Caravans", because of its prominence as a landmark. But he gave no philological explanation of these theories, and they are not now accepted. He also said that the Chagga tribe called it Kibo, meaning "snow".

Krapf said the Wakamba called it *Kima ja Jeu* "Mountain of Whiteness",i.e.the same meaning as Kima Ja Kegnia.

The word *Lima* means "mountain" in Swahili, and Ki- is normally a diminutive! Some people have tried to explain that Ki-may have other connotations (e.g. abnormality). But could not the diminutive be used either as a term of affection or as a form of bravado, to belittle any evil influence it might have. It is common for Africans humourously to call a large man "kidogo", meaning small.

The most likely derivation of *Njaro* is from the Swahili word "kung'aa" or "ngara" (to shine): but a derivation from a word "njaro" (water) has also been suggested.

According to people of the Chagga tribe today Kilimanjaro can be derived from the Chagga words *Kyalema Kyaro*, which mean "the climb/mountain that defeats many people". Kibo could either mean the top or up, it could however also be an exclaimation word without any special meaning.

The three old volcanic masses have african names - *Kibo, Ki-Mawenzi,* as it used to be called, and Shira. The meanings of these names are obscure, although Dutton said that Kibo meant elephant and Mawenzi a hunter. In view of their volcanic origin, the following old Chagga legend about Kibo and Mawenzi related by Rev Dr. R. Reusch in Ice-Cap No 1 is particularly interesting.

"Once, in ancient times, when both were still smoking their pipes, that of Mawenzi became extinguished. He went to his bigger but younger brother, Kibo, to borrow fire and received it. A short time later, while taking a nap, the fire in his pipe again went out. And again he went to borrow from Kibo. But this time the latter became very angry and thrashed him so terribly with his club that even one can see his bruised, battered and torn surface and sense his attitude of austerity, adopted after this unjust treatment. The Wachagga believe that Mawenzi is ashamed of its appearance, therefore covering its face with clouds at every opportunity. And it is indeed so, that one seldom sees Mawenzi without clouds".

Dr. Reusch also relates the legend of King Menelilk I of Abyssinia, the son of King Solomon and the Queen of Sheba. This Monarch, after conquering Eastern Africa, camped on his return journey on The Saddle of Kilimanjaro. Feeling death near, he climbed up to the crater of Kibo and disappeared into it with his slaves who were carrying his jewels and treasure. Here he sleeps forever. "But offspring of his family will arise and restore the old glory of Ethiopia, conquering all of the land to the Rufiji river. He will ascend Mt Kibo, find the jewels of Menelik I, among which will be the seal ring of Solomon which the old king has upon his finger. This ring he will put upon his own hand, and from this moment he will be endowed with the wisdom of Solomon. Also the heroic spirit of the old king will rest upon him. Thus the legend says".

Not unnaturally most of the names on Kilimanjaro are of German origin. Kaiser Wilhelm II, after whom Hans Meyer named the highest point of Kibo, this has now been changed to *Uhuru* (Freedom) Peak. But the name *Bismarck*, the Iron Chancellor of Prussia and architect of the German Empire, was commemorated in the lowest hut - now Mandara Hut, while the next hut, now called Horombo, was named after *Karl Peters*, the German explorer and arch-Imperialist. Another explorer and imperialist, *Wissman*, has a peak on Mawenzi named after him; he was sent by Bismarck to subdue the 1889 rebellion in Tanganyika and in 1895 and 1896 was Governor of German East Africa.

The glaciers of Kilimanjaro, like those of Mount Kenya are mostly named after scientists and geographers. Hans Meyer named the *Ratzel Glacier* after the well known German human geographer, others were named after E. von *Drygalski* and Polar explorer, geographer and glaciologist; *W. Credner* a geologist; A. *Penck* a geologist and glaciologist, and

A Heim a Swiss geologist and glaciologist are others who never visited Kilimanjaro but who have glaciers named after them. The *Rebmann* Glacier, on the other hand, is named after the first European to see the mountain, and the *Decken and Kersten* after the two Germans who were the first to reach the Alpine Zone of the mountain in 1862.

The peaks bear the names of climbers. The highest peak of Mawenzi was named after *Hans Meyer* by Oehler and Klute, the second peak now bears the name of Meyer's companion *Purtscheller*. Eisenmann was responsible for the names *Oehler Gully* and *Klute Peak*, and he also named Borchers Peak after one of the patrons of his expedition. *Lent*, who visited the mountain in the 1890's, has some minor peaks to the northwest of Kibo named after him. *Johannes Notch* is named after the District Officer, Moshi, who reached this point in 1898 and climbed the minor peak now called *Gillman's* after a prominent early member of the Mountain Club of East Africa. W. *Furtwangler's* climb of 1912 is the cause of the name of the crater glacier of Kibo. *Stella Point* is named after Mrs. Latham, who reached this point in 1925 with her husband, Kingsley *Latham* of the Mountain Club of South Africa. His relative, Dr. D. V. Latham, a founder member of the Mountain Club of East Africa, has the Mawenzi peak which he climbed after him; and G *Londt* another MCSA member, who first climbed South Peak Mawenzi, has the south ridge for Mawenzi named after him. *Elveda* (Shining) Point was named by Dr. Reuch, who also named *Leopard Point* and Notch after he found a frozen leopard there in 1926. The name of Reusch himself is given to the Inner (Ash Pit) Crater of Kibo.

Notes

Notes

Notes

Notes

Notes

Notes

Notes